Dundee CHANGING CULTURE

GOSLING

GOSLING

CLASSIC DESIGN FOR CONTEMPORARY INTERIORS

With contributions
by Stephen Calloway, Jean Gomm, Tim Gosling and Jürgen Huber

Foreword by Tim Knox,
Director, Sir John Soane's Museum, London

Photography by Ray Main

PRESTEL
MUNICH   BERLIN   LONDON   NEW YORK

Foreword

A direct link between today's designers and craftsmen and their counterparts in the past is an important one. The great buildings, interiors and furnishings that delight us today only do so because of the exceptional vision and skill of many extraordinary people – patrons, arbiters of taste, artists and craftsmen. It is heartening to see how many of the ideas of the past still resonate in the architecture and design of today.

Gosling as a company still aspires to the level of detail and quality that characterises the masters of the past. It maintains that vital dialogue, reviving in the luxurious houses, offices and hotels that feature in this beautiful book the spirit, stylishness and attention to detail that so distinguishes the work of William Kent, Robert Adam and Thomas Hope.

Tim Gosling has created a living museum at his design studio and home, enabling his discriminating clients to see and understand why historical rules, materials and proportions matter – very much continuing the dialogue that Sir John Soane had with his clients, and which governed the creation of the world-renowned museum I now curate in Lincoln's Inn Fields.

TIM KNOX, *Director, Sir John Soane's Museum, London*

I

The Classical Tradition

For those attuned to the glories of the past and full of the desire to create beautiful things themselves, the classical tradition inherited from the civilisations of ancient Egypt, Greece and Rome offers a fathomless source of instruction and inspiration. This book examines this legacy to reveal the way in which a passionate love of the classical architectural tradition has inspired and guided the creative career of a contemporary designer of furniture and interiors, Tim Gosling.

The connection between building, the creation of interior spaces and the making of furniture has from the most ancient times been intimate. One key to all this has been an understanding of the use of wood and the appreciation of its strengths and beauties as a material for builders and makers. The form of Greek temples and great civic edifices has been traced to the simple type of the 'primitive hut', its crude timber uprights gradually transformed over time into elegant columns of carefully cut stone, its crossbeams into lintel and architrave, the original elements of its construction and fixings recalled symbolically in an elaborate system of ornamental details and flourishes – the architectural Orders.

As a codification of scale and proportion, ornament and enrichment – or, curiously, when ornament and enrichment were not required, as an almost abstract set of principles – the Orders held everything together, providing sets of rules that whilst seeming absolute also remained endlessly adaptable.

In tracing the history of the transmission of the classical tradition down to our own era, perhaps the single most significant episode was the rediscovery by the Florentine Poggio Bracciolini, one of the most indefatigable and erudite classicists of the early Renaissance, of the hitherto lost works of the Roman architect Vitruvius. Marcus Vitruvius Pollio's *Ten Books on Architecture* were written probably around 15 BCE and constitute the only complete architectural treatise to have come down to us from ancient times. Vitruvius's writings revealed for the first time a comprehensive picture of the building methods of the ancients and evidence of their stylistic concerns; not surprisingly this precious text sparked the liveliest interest among scholars, artists and architectural practitioners when first made public in 1414.

In Italian scholarly circles Vitruvius became essential reading and for two centuries his works were digested, elaborated upon and imitated by a sequence of academic writers and architectural theorists. Daniel Barbaro's translation of Vitruvius's original Latin text, published in Venice in 1556 with extensive commentaries and illustrations by the talented young draughtsman and architect Andrea Palladio, became for their generation the standard edition. Another early 'Vitruvian', Leon Battista Alberti, in his *De re aedificatoria* was among the first to claim for

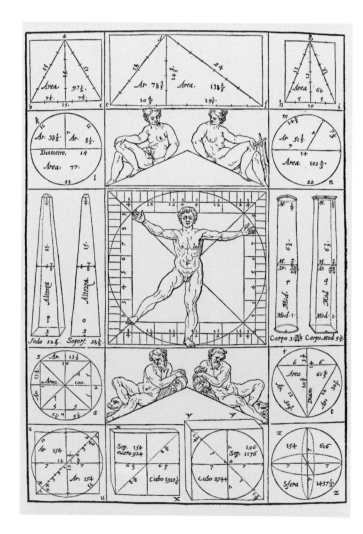

architecture a status as high as that of the established learned disciplines of rhetoric and poetry and those with which it shared a more obvious connection: geometry and music.

In an intellectual arena which delighted in complex and often highly speculative thought patterns, architectural theories concerning proportion came to be interwoven with more abstract notions of musical, linear and spatial harmony based on the subtle division of the Golden Section. Influenced by the speculations concerning the human form of anatomists and the more thoughtful or scientifically minded artists, such as Leonardo, Vincenzo Scamozzi, in his *L'Idea della Architettura universale* of 1615, elaborated a uniform system of mathematical ratios and visual harmonies founded upon the divine geometry of the ideal human figure. Whilst intended to be applied to the grandest of architectural projects, such theories also carried clear implications for designers and

makers in an era in which new kinds of private domestic spaces such as the *studiolo* and novel forms of furniture were developing rapidly.

Palladio's own treatise *I Quattro Libri dell'Architettura* of 1570 had, with a somewhat lighter touch, disseminated his theories of proportion and his love of geometrically complex but largely plain and unadorned forms far and wide. Whilst Palladio himself built only relatively small numbers of buildings in Venice and around Vicenza, his book became a cornerstone of architectural thinking for many years, and buildings in what came to be called the Palladian style spread as far afield as Russia and the Americas. In England in the early eighteenth century, during a period of unprecedented prosperity and confident expansion, Palladianism became the unchallenged architectural idiom of the dominant aristocratic, political and landowning classes.

The history of the classical tradition in England is essentially one of successive waves of influence reaching our shores. It was early in the sixteenth century during the reign of Henry VIII, who aspired above all to compete with his rival the French king François I as a European Renaissance prince, that new Italian architectural forms and motifs first began to appear. Seen at first in buildings and other fashionable artefacts associated with court circles, the 'Romane' fashion spread as the century progressed to the houses of aristocratic builders and even, more often than not barbarously misunderstood, to the carved oak furniture of stout Elizabethan gentlemen and yeomen farmers.

It is probably fair to say that the first British architect and designer fully to appreciate and understand the new Italian architecture, and to assimilate its ideas and its details sufficiently to build convincingly in the new style was Inigo Jones (1573–1652).

← Vincenzo Scamozzi, *I'Idea della Architettura universale*, 1615, Part I, Book I. The ideal proportions of the human body and basic geometric shapes.

→ Inigo Jones, Elevation for the penultimate design for the Banqueting House, Westminster, London, 1619–22.

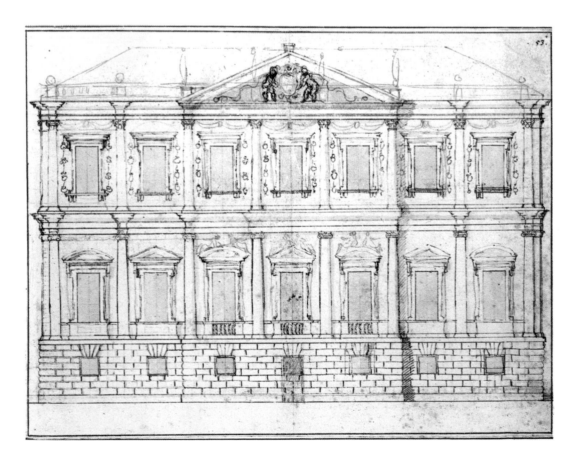

Jones both travelled to Italy seeing buildings at first hand and assiduously studied the works of Serlio and other more recent texts. He worked for James I, for whom he created the first great building in the true classical style in England, the Banqueting House, his masterpiece of 1619–22, as well as the Queen's House at Greenwich. It is significant that Jones was not only an architect but also, and very much in the Renaissance manner, a versatile designer of furniture, interiors and also settings and costumes for masques and other court entertainments. For this reason, in the breadth of his vision, he remains a model for designers today. As Tim Gosling says 'our story starts here'.

Throughout the rest of the seventeenth century in England, the majority of architectural practitioners remained amateurs. Even Sir Christopher Wren and Sir John Vanbrugh, the greatest of these 'learned and ingenious gentlemen' were essentially self-taught. Wren, as an Oxford academic, had studied Vitruvius as a classical text, but it was his visits to Paris and Rome that opened his eyes to the new European baroque architecture. Gosling cites Wren's celebrated library at Trinity College, Cambridge, as well as numerous details in his London churches as seminal influences. If Wren's architecture and design was essentially cerebral, his two closest associates, Nicholas Hawksmoor, his sometime assistant and collaborator, and John Vanbrugh both introduced new elements of heady baroque theatricality into English architecture. In Hawksmoor's case it is revealed most clearly in his daring use of towers to dramatise church or college structures; in Vanbrugh it is to be seen and relished most in the extraordinarily powerful massing of the blocks of his great country houses, Blenheim Palace and Castle Howard with their unforgettable sky-lines of bristling obelisks and vases.

The fruitful association at this time of Richard Boyle, 3rd Earl of Burlington and the painter-turned-architect William Kent proved to be one of the greatest collaborations between a patron of vision and a designer of genius. Burlington's grand villa at Chiswick proclaimed his architectural allegiances by placing statues of Palladio and Inigo Jones to the right and left of the portico. Internally, the villa — a pleasure pavilion on the grandest scale, which was never intended to be lived in — revealed the sophistication with which Kent could create furniture with an architectural character, and place it within interior schemes in which all the elements were integrated to an unprecedented degree. This ability to marry grandiose effect and attention to small detail continually delights the eye in Kent's finest interior ensembles such as those of Holkham Hall or Houghton, and equally in individual pieces of furniture such as a bookcase or chair, a candle stand or a simple plinth on which to display a Grand Tour treasure.

← Christopher Wren, The Wren library at Magdalen College, Cambridge, 1676–86.

→ A bay of the Wren library showing reading tables and reading stand attributed to Christopher Wren.

→→ A sketch design of the reading tables and reading stand attributed to Christopher Wren.

The major trend of the later eighteenth-century architectural confraternity was towards an increasing professionalism. The careers of the three greatest neo-classical architects of the period, James 'Athenean' Stuart, Sir William Chambers and Robert Adam reveal a certain similarity of aim and achievement. All three had immersed themselves deeply in studies of the architecture of the ancient world and all three found ways in which to apply this knowledge to the creation of interiors and the kinds of furniture required in modern civic and domestic situations. Of the specialist furniture makers of the day none enjoys a greater reputation, even to this day, than Thomas Chippendale. Working for many of the most important patrons of his day, Chippendale exemplifies the trajectory of the talented craftsman who rose to the status of designer and highly successful contractor. His position at the cutting-edge of his trade was cemented by the publication of a book of his own designs, the celebrated *Gentleman and Cabinet-Maker's Director*. Published in three editions between 1754 and 1762, this highly influential pattern-book spanned the crucial mid-century development in furniture design away from the fanciful elaboration of the rococo and towards a more severe and 'regular' neo-classical style.

One of the most remarkable changes in social life in the late eighteenth century was a marked movement away from formality. The greatest consequence of this trend both in social and design terms was a novel search for comfort and softness in interiors and the creation of many entirely new forms of furnishings. Old-style rooms of parade and formal parlours were replaced with comfortable morning rooms, multi-purpose libraries and new kinds of charmingly informal drawings-rooms. Sumptuously upholstered pieces of furniture such as chaises longues and Grecian couches were placed in relation to novel items such as tea-tables and ladies' sewing-tables. John Nash, the favourite architect of the Prince Regent, later George IV, was the master of this new style. His interiors for the Prince in the Brighton Pavilion combined exotic colour with the most profligate use of rich materials; in some ways this was a trend that would continue to define the interiors of a small elite of extravagant patrons in America as well as in England and France well into the twentieth century.

By comparison with Nash's lavish interiors, those created by the other great architect of the Regency period Sir John Soane seem in a way restrained. Soane's genius lay in the ordering of architectural space, the opening of unexpected vistas from room to room and the multiplication of views and transformation of light by the use of mirrors. Soane's personal extravagance lay in the collecting of antiquities and curiosities (as well as sculpture, drawings, paintings, furniture and books). His own house, laid

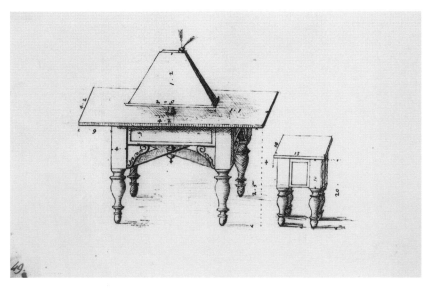

out as a private museum, celebrated the legacy of the classical world, but used myriad architectural conceits to create the most innovative and inventive domestic spaces and decorative interiors of his day. One of Soane's more famous pupils, Sir Robert Smirke is another of Tim Gosling's heroes, celebrated for his imposing design for the British Museum.

With the waning of the neo-classicical influence as the nineteenth century progressed, other styles such as gothic increasingly came to the fore. The Victorian interior was characterised by its unprecedented density of furnishing as well as by the overwhelming reliance it placed upon historicising styles of furniture and decoration. Even the furniture designers of the Aesthetic movement and reformers of the 1870s such as Charles Lock Eastlake, Christopher Dresser and Bruce Talbert conformed essentially to this pattern. E. W. Godwin, who took many of his

models from Japan and especially from ancient Greece, was one of a few architect–designers to create spare, elegant rooms and furnish them with unornamented pieces built upon slender lines. However, by the end of the century inventive spirits such as Sir Edwin Lutyens were again breathing new life into the traditional classical forms, playing erudite games with an architecture full of witty allusions to the past.

The rise of Modernism in the early years of the twentieth century did not, as might have been expected, mean that all interest in the styles of the past was expunged and nor did it bring about the demise of the classical tradition. Classically trained architects such as Sir Albert Richardson continued to work using the Orders and ancient canons of proportions and detailing. Others, such as Sir Owen Williams adapted classical principles and applied them to the creation of new types of structure created with novel materials, such as the Dorchester

Hotel or his innovative Daily Express Building in London, an Art Deco extravagance clad in black Vitrolite. For designers such as Tim Gosling who from time to time wish or are required by the nature of the commission to work in a more contemporary idiom, three great figures from the pioneering or heroic phase of International Modernism stand as inspiration: Ludwig Mies van der Rohe, Walter Gropius and Le Corbusier. Mies claimed that he sought to establish an architecture fully representative of modern times and as much the natural expression of the age as the classical and gothic styles had been. The emphasis in this twentieth-century architectural style was on extreme clarity and simplicity, and his buildings made the most daring use of modern materials such as industrial steel and plate glass to define interior spaces.

In general terms the trend in England in those creative inter-war years was towards

← Sir John Soane,
The Library-Dining Room
in Sir John Soane's house,
London, 1798.

→ The Breakfast Room in
Sir John Soane's house.

a gentler Modernism based on the observance of classical proportion in buildings increasingly stripped of any historical decorative detail either externally or internally. By contrast French designers of interiors and furniture makers such as André Arbus explored the use of novel design motifs, but worked with ever-richer materials that evoked the luxuries of the past. For contemporary designers, such as Tim Gosling, both these strategies can offer exciting potential.

These days relatively few major buildings are erected in a 'correct' classical style, adhering to the precise proportional dictates of the orders and enriched with carved decoration following the ancient models. Indeed, most contemporary buildings that are designed this way tend to be small, private and often frivolous adornments for the gardens and parks of indulgent landowners. However, every year vast numbers of new buildings all over the world, including large-scale, seemingly 'free' ultra-modernist structures and many high-tech sky-scrapers which subtly reference the three-part division of the classical column into base, shaft and capital, still conform either imperceptibly or perhaps even unconsciously to many of the proportional canons of the classical manner. Paradoxically, the fact that so much of our furnishings and interiors, and so many new buildings seem so deliberately free-form, and yet observe – however obliquely – 'the rules', serves to point up and strengthen the assertion that the classical tradition remains even today a pervasive, potent and positive influence on the way we choose to live.

↑ Gosling fitted library
constructed in sycamore.

→ The oculus in a private
library in English sycamore
with a Venetian reliquary, the
back section inlaid with
London plane (lacewood).

2

Space, Scale and Light

In the second chapter of Book I of his *Ten Books on Architecture* Vitruvius described the key factors contributing to good design as *order* and *arrangement*; *eurythmy* and *symmetry*; *propriety* and *economy*.

Order for Vitruvius meant correctness in the choice and scaling of the individual members, parts and details of the edifice in relation to the whole, together with a regard for the overall form. This in turn led to his notion of *arrangement* which concerned the proper placing of all the elements, again stressing the correspondence of the parts to the whole with a view not only to function or use, but also to the creation of an elegance that pleased the eye. Vitruvius tells us that the tools by which the architect or designer achieves *order* and *arrangement* are the ground plan, the elevation and the perspective; a clear injunction, still relevant today, that drawing remains essential to the design process.

The architectural Orders lay down 'rules' which guide the architect or designer towards *order* and *arrangement*. By proposing an ideal template for scaling and proportioning every part of a building, the Orders also formed the basis for *eurythmy*, the beauty and sense of aesthetic pleasure that came about through long experience by architects in the ordering of the parts to create rhythm and visual harmony. Closely related, too, was Vitruvius's notion of *symmetry*, by which he meant not, as we now tend to define it, the placing of elements in a mirror-image arrangement, but rather a much more abstract ideal of harmonious agreement of each of the parts, one with another, and all in relation to the whole.

Under the rubric of *propriety* Vitruvius brought together ideas both of employment of the correct building type and correctness and appropriateness of plan, form and detail. Defining his final principle, *economy*, Vitruvius strikes a particularly topical note. Whilst impressing upon architects and designers the importance of employing the right — and

appropriately rich — materials in any project, he also stresses the need always to favour those that can be locally sourced and the necessity of seeking clever alternatives to those that cannot to be obtained without undue trouble and disproportionate expense.

Vitruvius summarised these principles, saying that edifices of all types must be built 'with due regard to Durability, Convenience and Beauty'. This simple injunction was taken up by Sir Henry Wotton, a gentleman-amateur whose *Elements of Architecture* of 1624 was the first important architectural treatise published in England. Following Vitruvius closely, Wotton wrote that 'in Architecture as in all other Operative Arts, the end must direct the Operation. The end is to build well. Well building hath three Conditions: Commoditie, Firmness and Delight'. From this straightforward statement he then proceeds to make an intriguingly subtle observation concerning the third condition, Delight:

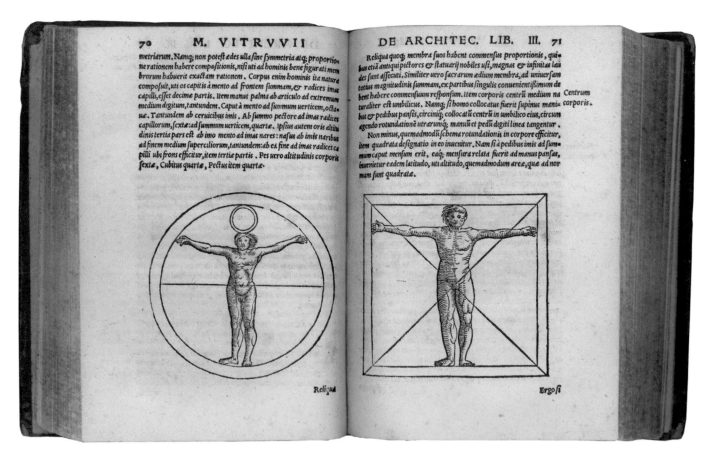

⇐ Leonardo da Vinci, after Vitruvius, *The Proportions of the Human Figure*, c.1490.

← Marcus Vitruvius Pollio, A wood-cut engraving of the Vitruvian man from *Ten Books on Architecture*. This first German edition was printed in 1543, with the plates based on those of the Como edition of 1521.

In truth a sound piece of good Art, where the Materials be but ordinarie stone, without any garnishment of sculpture, doe yet ravish the Beholder, (and he knows not how) by a secret Harmony in the Proportions. And this indeede is that end, at which we should ayme even in the privatest workes.

Wotton clearly knew his Italian sources well, for much of the work of the major architectural theorists of the fifteenth and sixteenth centuries was concerned with the elaboration of complex systems of proportion, sizing and scale.

One of the most important theories of 'secret harmony' in proportions concerned the so-called Golden Mean or Golden Section, the division of a line into two unequal parts, whereby the shorter length bears the same relation to the longer as the longer to the whole (the actual ratio is 1:1.618, as first pointed out by Fibonacci in 1202). This division, enshrined by the Ancients, was held to have an almost mystical or numerological significance. Not only did it form the basis of a system of visual proportion; it was also held, because of the relationship between notes produced by an 'open' string and one 'stopped' at the point of the Golden Section, to be a fundamental building block in systems of musical harmony. And today designers such as Gosling still find the Golden Section an important tool for ravishing the eye of the beholder.

A second fundamental basis for all design concerns the more precise application of scale and proportion which dictates sizing. Vitruvius drew attention (as an aspect of his principle of *symmetry*) to the idea that the human body offered a perfect example of utility and harmonious beauty in the relation of the parts to the whole. From ancient times, whole systems of interrelated measurements were calculated from the lengths of the finger, arm, foot, head and their relation to the total height of the adult male frame. All the enduring measurements of human scale: the ancient *cubit*, the Renaissance *braccia* (based on the forearm) and our own *foot* have been thus derived, whilst many of the larger, architectural units of mensuration evolved from logical multiplications of them.

Such systems of measurement and the theories of harmony, proportion and sizing which flowed from them were given impetus during the middle years of the Renaissance by unprecedented advances in anatomy and anthropometrical studies (the measuring of human and animal forms). One of Leonardo's most beautiful pen drawings shows a naked man inscribed within the geometrical figures of circle and perfect square. This celebrated image is the finest depiction of the 'Vitruvian Man', the symbolic representation of Vitruvius's concept of a system of proportion based on the human form.

→ Inigo Jones (attrib.), Design for a cabinet, c.1636. W. Grant Keith wrote in *Some Hitherto Unknown Drawings by Inigo Jones* in *The Burlington Magazine for Connoisseurs* (vol. 22, no. 118, January 1913): 'It supplies us for the first time with an example of Inigo Jones's work as a designer of furniture… The design, of very fine proportions, is treated on architectural lines… The treatment of the upper portion of the cabinet is analogous in certain features to various overmantel designs from the same hand. The broken pediment with the cartouche in its centre supported by *amorini* was a favourite theme with Inigo Jones …This cabinet design is valuable as showing that the furniture which was to occupy his interiors also came in for consideration. It seems more than probable that in his houses of importance Jones must have had a controlling hand in the design of the furniture, of the chief pieces at any rate.'

On a more mundane level, the idea of a system in which man is 'the measure of all things' gives rise to a pragmatic approach to the design and making of furniture in which standardised heights and sizes have become more or less fixed because the human frame has changed very little over centuries (we are today somewhat taller and more heavily built than our more recent ancestors, but the increases are barely significant). For example, once the Roman fashion for eating in a reclining position on couches gave way in the West to sitting at a table, the standard height of such tables became fixed through convenience at about 31 inches (73–75 cm), whilst the standard for either the rudest plank benches or the seats of the most sophisticated of dining chairs has remained constant at around 17 inches (42.5–45 cm). Eighteenth- and nineteenth-century designers such as Thomas Hepplewhite almost invariably worked with such measurements; Tim Gosling observes them today, using

them also as a basis for sizing other pieces such as console tables, the height of which is not strictly dictated by use to the same degree. Needless to say, the height of the backs of chairs, which is a matter of visual rather than practical consideration, has fluctuated wildly with fashion, reaching a height of exaggeration in about 1690–1700 that has been equalled only once and briefly by Charles Rennie Mackintosh in 1900.

As a key aspect of scale in design, sizing is very intimately connected to obvious practical considerations. By comparison, space and its disposition by the architect are far freer and more abstract concerns, affected by the unique interaction of the designer's intention and the individual viewer's experience. All buildings enclose space. We measure these interior spaces, whether in a cathedral, a library or a tiny room by our own human scale, but the calculating and ingenious designer can play all manner of games with our perception of actual or

apparent volumes and also of 'negative space', the all-important empty areas between architectural elements or pieces of furniture. In the more distant past, grandiose buildings such as temples and palaces relied upon massive scale (as well as richness of decoration) to create a sense of awe in the beholder. With the growth of the importance of private domestic space from the sixteenth century and the consequent distinction which increasingly arose between public and private space, more subtle manipulations of the experience of the visitor became possible.

In Baroque palaces and the grander houses of the seventeenth and early eighteenth centuries the planning of space was crucial. The progression from one space to the next became of the greatest significance. The theatrical arranged enfilade of rooms, one leading into the next, became an overt statement of the relative status of the owner and those who wished to approach him. The importunate supplicant or

← This Gosling watercolour by Marianne Topham, shows evenly spaced torcheres on one side and, on the other side standing in front of the windows, bookcases which accentuate these apertures to give a sense of symmetry and eurythmy. Interior design by Anouska Hempel Designs.

→ Gosling watercolour by Marianne Topham of the Goring Hotel Bar.

welcome, distinguished visitor progressed first through the most public spaces, through rooms carefully calibrated by increasing levels of both privacy and richness of furnishing. Eventually, only the most honoured guest reached the final antechamber and was perhaps ushered into the inner sanctum of the bedchamber.

In medieval times, the furnishings owned by peripatetic kings or rich landowners were, for the most part, portable; tapestries for the walls, tables and chairs and the master's bedstead and its hangings were constantly carried from one place to another. It is, therefore, no accident that the idea of the permanently furnished house and an interest in architecturally planned gardens arose at much the same time, first in Renaissance Italy but spreading rapidly throughout Europe in the sixteenth century. It was in Italy too that architects – or painters and designers – seem first to have turned their attention to the creation of pieces of furniture intended for

specific positions within carefully contrived interiors.

Tim Gosling traces the lineage of his design ideals to this era of exciting development and, perhaps even more specifically, to the moment at which these Italianate influences first made themselves felt in England. Some of the very first architectural furniture was created by Francis Cleyn, a German working in the brilliant circle of Inigo Jones, for the once splendid, but now lost London mansion of Holland House. Rough sketches by Jones himself survive that show his interest extending beyond giving the design of the wall treatments and chimneypieces for rooms to that of individual pieces of furniture. His enterprising nephew John Webb certainly also drew designs, including one for an elaborate bed intended to stand in a great niche in the bedchamber of Charles II at Greenwich Palace.

The provision of some specific types of furnishing naturally remained to a

considerable degree the preserve of the architect. Libraries and galleries offered the designer opportunities to build up a grandiose effect through the repetition of forms. The Vitruvian notions of order and eurythmy governed the placing of bookcases, rows of columns or vistas of serried ranks of pedestals supporting classical busts or vases. Tim Gosling has repeatedly made use of such devices in many of his design schemes, whether on a large or more intimate scale. Like many designers he has a particular liking for the effect of carefully contrived shelves for the display of collections of objects and readily subscribes to that most delightful idea that 'books do furnish a room'.

The seventeenth century was an era of palace building and furnishing on an heroic scale. The idea of the fully architectural interior became crucial, with space manipulated to dramatic effect through the placing of the elements, through repetition, reflection in mirrors and by the use of

materials that played with light. The notion of the ensemble of furnishings grew in importance and display became ever more lavish. Louis XIV and his rivals and imitators commissioned vast suites of furniture, often made of heavy chased silver. Designers such as Charles le Brun, who had a painter's eye for placing, and especially Daniel Marot, the master of ornate embellishment, increasingly played with the idea of forming groups of related pieces of furniture which worked together to increase the cumulative effect of the interior.

Two of these groupings of furniture pieces attained a curious canonical status, repeated in the grandest of palace rooms but imitated, in lesser materials, even in the far more modest houses of the rising merchant classes. The first of these 'sets' of pieces has come to be called a 'triad'; it consisted of a table flanked by a symmetrically placed pair of candle-stands. Lavish triads in silver can be seen at Knole, their form precisely echoed

in simpler lacquered wood examples in the collection of original furnishings preserved at Ham House. Because such a triad grouping was often placed on the pier between two openings, it became natural to associate the triad group with the mirror which it was at this time customary to hang between windows. A version of such an arrangement, with a small looking-glass set upon the table, gave rise to another canonical or classic grouping, the dressing-table. Gradually the association of the pier-table and pier-glass gained in popularity and became one of the most widespread features of the classic architectural interior. It is a form which Gosling uses often, sometimes in a directly historical manner, in homage to another of his classical heroes, William Kent, but also sometimes in a more subtly allusive way, merely hinting at traditional grandeur.

From Renaissance times architects and designers have delighted in the use of all manner of visual games to create curious and

pleasingly deceptive effects. The eye and the intellect take pleasure, it seems, in being thus deceived. The use of painted *trompe l'oeil* is just one possible resource for the designer, but the building of actual *trompe-l'oeil* architecture became a favourite conceit of architects during the Mannerist period (1520–80). One of the finest examples of such trickery in stone remains the extraordinary vaulted corridor of the Palazzo Spada in Rome where Borromini miraculously contrived by the use of falsified scale and perspective to conjure within the space of a few yards the illusion of a monumental vista of columns and vaults.

A similar use of contrast between the expected scale of things and reality was exploited by William Kent in his interiors and furnishings of the celebrated villa at Chiswick which he created for, and in collaboration with, his patron Richard Boyle, 3rd Earl of Burlington. Never intended to be used as a residence, but rather as a place for

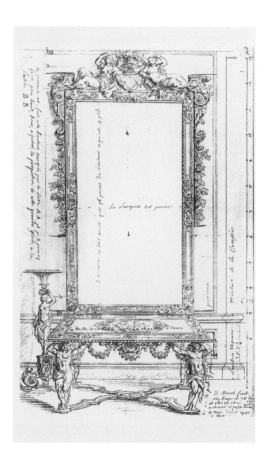

←← Daniel Marot's design for a triad to be set up at Het Loo, near Apeldoorn, the Netherlands, c.1684.

← A French silver triad set in the King's Room at Knole House in Sevenoaks in Kent, designed in 1676–81.

→ Chairs in the Gallery at Chiswick House in London by William Kent (c.1726–29) are deliberately scaled down to match the small size of the rooms.

entertainment in the gardens by day and elegant soirées and suppers in candlelit rooms by night, Chiswick House was a brilliant *jeu d'esprit*, and the pre-eminent statement of the English Palladian ideal as conceived by Burlington. Though hardly a small building, the planning was correct but relatively compact, the rooms relatively modest in scale though most richly ornamented in the best architectural taste. Here Kent's brilliant conceit was to make all the furnishings just a little smaller than the norm, thereby giving the illusion that every space was larger than it was in reality. In the hands of a master such manipulation of space and scale can be entrancing, adding a new layer to our appreciation of correct architectural form and detail. Knowing the rules, but also knowing how to break them can be one of the most essential parts of the mindset of the successful designer.

————

It is perhaps significant that our great classical architectural traditions originated in Greece and were further refined by the Romans in Italy, places where clear, strong, directional sunlight is the norm and all details appear crisply delineated. The heavily ornamented cornice, the interplay of metopes and triglyphs, the deeply moulded arch and the massive fluted column all seem contrived to 'read' most forcefully in bright sunshine. Transplanted to cloudy England their effect is inevitably diminished. Certainly in the eighteenth century when speculative theories concerning cultural identity began to be discussed, it was often observed that the cool, misty northern light had by contrast naturally fostered the development of the gothic style.

Long before the influence of the painterly representation of light in rooms had become a factor in the perception of architectural interiors (one thinks of the melodramatic scenes of Caravaggio, or the

quieter, more reflective paintings of Vermeer and Rembrandt), designers had played with the many varied possibilities of light. In Greek temples the progress from the brilliance of outdoor light, through the dramatically contrasting shadows of the central columniated space and finally into the mysterious darkness of the inner sanctum was precisely modulated. In the cathedrals of the north light was refracted through vast windows of painted glass to fall on often highly coloured stonework. In a building such as San Marco in Venice, which owed most to Byzantine tradition, light shafted through small openings and illuminated the glittering gold tesserae of mosaics in patches that emerged from an almost unfathomably vast, gloomy space. In early twelfth-century Paris, Abbot Suger of Saint-Denis spent a lifetime enriching his church with opulent altar vessels, vestments and other rich objects. Obsessively observing the effects of light falling upon gold, on enamel or on silk, he

developed a specialised, idiosyncratic Latin vocabulary that included numerous terms to characterise the effulgence of light on each different material. In all these cases, the effect of light upon surfaces was crucial; the materials employed changed those effects according to their individual properties.

For centuries the quality of light in domestic interiors changed remarkably little. The rich man burned many candles of fine wax, while the poor made do with the spluttering, stinking flame of the tallow-dip or the glimmer of the rush-light. In the seventeenth and eighteenth centuries the grandest occasions were enlivened by the light of crystal chandeliers and wall sconces; but even by the time of Jane Austen the opulence of a social occasion was still measured by the number of candles burning. Only as the nineteenth century progressed did new technology bring significant advances. First came the new oil-burners, lamps such as Argand's patent with its bright flame created

by whale-oil or crushed colza in a pressurised reservoir. Next came gas, the extraordinary brilliance of which entranced Sir Walter Scott when he installed it in his gothick pile at Abbotsford. Towards the latter end of the century incandescent electric bulbs powered by private generators began to appear, though it would be well into the twentieth century before the revolution was complete and most homes were lit by electric light supplied by a central power source.

Present-day lighting technology is now so sophisticated that almost any effect is possible. Where individual pieces of furniture were once dimly lit and blended into the room, now it is possible to use spot-lights with customised cut lenses which allow a piece to be illuminated with no 'spill' of light; such focus demands of the designer and maker the highest quality of materials, detailing and finish. Tim Gosling exploits to the full the possibilities which various kinds of light source offer to the

contemporary designer. At one extreme he uses wall-lights calibrated to provide a brightness of one lumen (the power of a single candle) and wired to flicker like a natural candle-flamer; at the other, some projects require the most sophisticated, programmable light systems that new technology can make available.

Gosling summarises the four main ways in which he uses and manipulates light in his projects as floating; sourced; reflecting; or those based upon surface treatments such as burnishing and gilding. Floating light relies upon the use of materials such as glass, or in modern times acrylic, to give the impression of floating or semi-transparency. Light shines through, into or underneath and around a piece, making it, and the area in which it is placed, seem lighter. Whilst seemingly thoroughly modern in concept, such ideas reference the use of precious material such as rock-crystal in seventeenth century objects for the wunderkammer, or the glass furniture and

← Gosling sketch by Marianne Topham of the Goring Hotel Drawing Room. To create an illusion of height the gilded ceiling is lit to reflect light into the eglomise panels around the room; the red silk walls by Pierre Frey reflect the light and create a sense of space.

→ Sir John Soane, detail of the Library-Dining Room in Sir John Soane's House, London, 1798. This was painted his favourite Pompeian red.

staircases supplied to Indian maharajahs in the nineteenth century by the firm of Osler.

The inclusion of a light source within the piece itself is a new and exciting technique. Here the possibilities include drilling to let light in, the channelling of natural light, or the incorporation of integral lighting as a design feature.

The use of reflected light in interiors has a long history. Materials such as mirror or eglomise (reverse-painted glass) have been employed since the seventeenth century to reflect and magnify light. Whilst the most celebrated and grandiose example of the use of mirror must be Louis XIV's Hall of Mirrors at Versailles, looking-glass has often been employed in more novel and subtle ways. Sir John Soane was perhaps the greatest exponent of this, employing narrow strips of mirror to multiply the perspectives of small rooms as well as little convex mirrors strategically placed around skylights to reflect light and amplify space.

In addition to the use of mirrors and glass surfaces, Gosling also exploits the underrated possibilities of wood itself, utilising the qualities of the grain to create tricks of light. Wood itself, because of its organic structure, has many curious properties. The grain of the wood reflects light in much the same way as the pile of a fabric, in one direction. This property is used to design advantage by the technique of book-matching, the placing side-by-side of veneers with grains running at different angles. This in turn sometimes gives a sort of lenticular effect. When, for example, one views a table-top from one angle certain areas or segments of the veneered surface look dark and lustrous next to lighter areas; move to another position and the darker and lighter parts appear to alternate.

Gosling's use of carving, gilding and burnishing and other reflective surfaces such as lacquer is at once highly traditional and innovative. French gilders in the eighteenth century knew well how to maximise the effect of gilding, playing up the differences of finish to balance the light from a side source or to create a flickering play of light that scatters across the carved detail of a pier-glass frame or boiserie panel. Similarly, burnishing of the gold, either uniformly or to different degrees depending on the position of the piece, can create a shimmer and an impression of emanating light. Unusually for a designer today Gosling collaborates closely with craftsmen in the workshop to exploit all the possibilities of these age-old techniques. For him, the preservation and practise of the old skills is an essential element that goes hand in hand with cutting-edge design.

→→ Programmable spotlights built into a garden design for a Gosling private client. The garden was designed by Andy Sturgeon (with Christian Garnett Partners, construction by ISG). This shows the ability to create rhythm using light sources by breaking up the curve of the wall and accentuating the window arches.

← ↙ Spotlights built into a bedhead by Gosling. The Goring Hotel, London.

→ An example of light designed to mimic the light source in an artwork. The entire space was constructed around the photograph by Hiroshi Sugimoto of a waxwork museum in Holland which represents in physical form the paintings of Vermeer.

This radially slip-matched dining table by Gosling is constructed entirely in one wood, American walnut. To create patterning and the use of light within the wood the direction of grain has been changed. Design by Millais Interior Design.

A bookcase by Gosling constructed in herringbone inlaid ripple sycamore. Only one in every twenty sycamore trees is a 'ripple' – such a rare wood has an exceptional iridescent quality in the wood grain. This sycamore contrasts internally with the walnut which makes the bookcase appear deeper.

← Gilded frames at the Goring Hotel, London. Red lacquer walls help to bounce light around the room, accentuated by the frame inside a frame – an idea Tim Gosling first saw used in auction houses.

→ This mirror took over ten months to hand carve, gesso, gild and burnish. The gilding on the mirror is balanced according to the directional light streaming in from the window on the left. Design by Millais Interior Design.

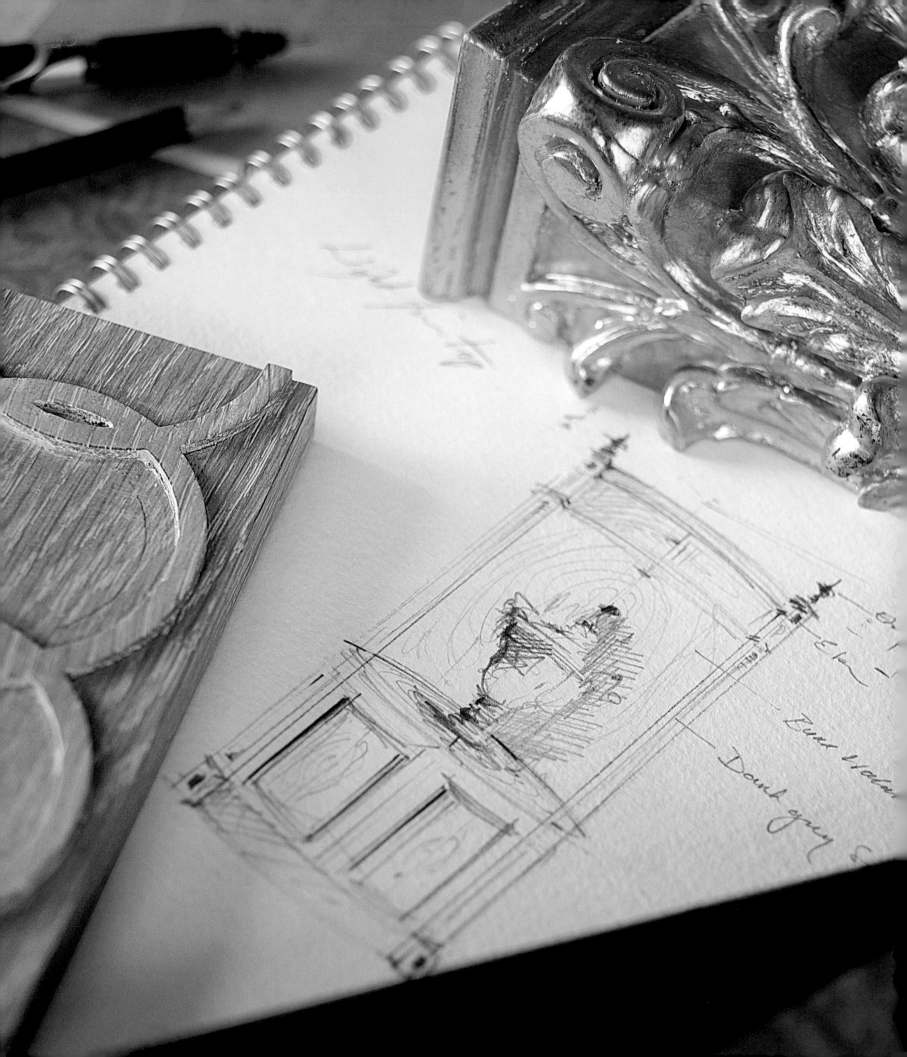

3

Commissioning

In the past every object of any importance, whether a throne, a table for a ducal hall or a set of expensively embroidered bed-hangings, was made to order. People of substance commissioned their furnishings, just as they ordered their clothes to be made to their specific requirement, specifying the cut and materials with regard to prevailing fashion, but essentially according to their own taste. Only in the late seventeenth century, with the emergence of a new and increasingly numerous and influential middle-class and the first tentative beginnings of commercial production did a gradual shift occur whereby growing numbers of people expected to buy many things 'over the counter', accepting what was on offer and having no say in the processes of design and making.

By the middle years of the eighteenth century many types of goods of the middling sort were easily available 'ready-made', and even some relatively expensive luxury goods used in furnishing, such as mirrors or printed wallpapers, could be purchased in the fashionable shops of London tradesmen. At the upper end of the scale it naturally continued to be the practise of the aristocracy and the richer mercantile classes to bespeak every element of their furnishings from specialist suppliers according to the dictates of an architect. A clear distinction thus arose between ordering goods (and waiting for them) and the activity which we now call shopping. Our present-day model of the practise of commissioning, with all its connotations of exclusivity and prestige, effectively dates from this era and remains little changed.

The taste of elite society in the eighteenth century was largely formed by the Grand Tour. Young men of position and wealth were sent to visit the great cities of Europe, to see at first hand the remains of ancient civilisation in Italy and to gain polish from contact with the best continental society. A second important aspect of the Grand Tour was the opportunity it afforded rich young men to buy and bring home classical sculptures, vases and other objects of varying degrees of authenticity offered by the more or less trustworthy dealers who plied their trade in great numbers. Many fine houses in England still retain collections begun in this way and displayed in the neo-classical taste which the Grand Tour dictated as the prevailing fashionable standard throughout the period from around 1660 to the coming of the railways in the 1840s.

Rome, as the fount of the classical tradition, was also a magnet for young architects eager to imbibe at first hand the lessons of Antiquity. In the case of Robert Adam his experience of Rome and the contacts he made there formed the entire basis of his subsequent distinguished career as architect and designer. Realising that he could not hope to establish a successful practise in Scotland Adam returned after several years study and set up in London in

← James Adam, Sketch proposal for a domed sculpture gallery at the rear of 75 (later 76) Lower Grosvenor Street, London, c.1767.

→ Robert Adam, Carved and gilt-wood torcheres from the drawing room at Luton Hoo, 1772.

1758, where his unrivalled first-hand knowledge of the classical style earned him the soubriquet of 'Bob the Roman'. In his establishment in Lower Grosvenor Street he surrounded himself with casts, antique fragments, prints and drawings to serve both as inspiration and to dazzle connoisseurs and potential clients.

Initially, Adam had a number of Scottish champions who recommended his skills and so helped to secure his first few commissions. These in turn led to others, a process of 'word-of-mouth' publicity that remains even today one of the essential ways in which the designer secures new work.

Adam's commissioning process was efficient, well thought-out and businesslike. The first step, following initial discussions, was the creation of drawings for the client; these were sometimes made by Adam himself, but often by one of his many draughtsmen, all of whose work was as a matter of course recorded as Adam's property. Such drawings were often done in duplicate: the first was for the client who paid a fee and kept the design even if it went unexecuted; the second was retained for the office for reference, as a marketing tool to show other clients or to be sent out to elicit estimates from craftsmen such as Adam's preferred plasterer, Joseph Rose. Once clients had agreed to go ahead they were expected to pay a 'surveyor's fee', typically of four or five per cent, which included almost everything except the occasional 'drawing at large' that might be required to complete a project.

As was customary, Adam usually designed the fixed and wall furniture to be included in his interior projects – pieces such as bookcases, pier-glasses and console tables – together with some other free-standing but essentially architectural items such as pedestals, torcheres and lampstands. He did not typically design the more utilitarian furniture which was normally ordered straight from the furniture makers, but even in these cases Adam expected to be consulted as an arbiter of taste and elegance. When he did give the designs for specific pieces these would be sent for execution to his favoured furniture makers, Chippendale, Ince and Mayhew or Linnell.

Adam's design ethos was based on the Vitruvian virtues of order, proportion and harmony of the parts with the whole. He also believed in the need to combine utility and beauty. More than a century later, William Morris, a medievalist inspired by the intricate organic forms of the gothic and thus stylistically poles apart from Adam's neo-classical sensibility, would codify an essentially similar philosophy in his famous phrase: 'have nothing in your houses that you do not know to be useful or believe to be beautiful'. This is a lofty ideal to which architects, designers and their all-important patrons have constantly reverted.

← Robert Adam, An engraving of a pair of torcheres designed for the Earl of Bute for Luton Hoo, Bedfordshire, 1772.

→ Robert Adam, Study of a tripod table, 1755. A tripod table dug up while Adam was in Herculaneum, which he sketched there and then.

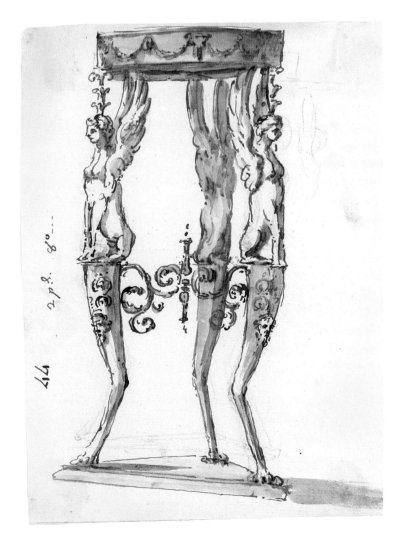

↑ Robert Adam, The Eating
Room at Osterley Park, with
mahogany lyre-back chairs
(part of a suite of 12) by
John Linnell, c.1767.

→ A set of quartetto tables
by Gosling in stained mazur
birch with lyre motifs in
brass. The lyre strings are
made from milled brass and
diminish in number with the
reduction in size of each lyre
table in the set.

One might imagine that the experience of commissioning fine furniture in Georgian England would be unrecognisable to present-day designers, but in fact, the essence of the process is almost unchanged. For Gosling, the act of commissioning anything, from a single piece of furniture to an entire building is still a privileged one, and the relationship of the client and designer continues to be a collaboration based on a mutual appreciation of beauty and classical design concepts.

The first step, as it would have been with Robert Adam and any of his wealthy patrons, is a conversation between designer and client – a pooling of ideas and inspirations – leading to hand-drawn sketches, rough drafted on the spot, usually in the space for which the commission is to be made, and then redrawn later for presentation. Creating sketch drawings by hand gives both the designer and client a critical understanding of the project, and sensitivity to scale,

proportion and rhythm – three vital elements of the creative design process. It also allows the designer and client to explore more personal elements related to how the individual client interacts with the space and the pieces under discussion.

After the sketch, the next step is the painting of a water-colour which serves the purpose of helping the project come to life for the client. It is extremely important to create a visual representation at this stage as each party will have a different concept of the language used, especially today as much of the terminology of cabinet-making has disappeared from our lexicon. One such example is when discussing the subtle visual differences between a bolection moulding as opposed to an ogee moulding; it is essential to have a visual aid to appreciate the impact of each.

Apart from providing samples of wood and fabric, this would have been the final presentation to the clients of Adam, Stuart

and Kent before they committed to the proposed projects. Now however, with the aid of 3-D Computer Modelling programmes, it is possible to lift the design from the page and show the client their commission from different vantage points and aspects, and also to reproduce the effects of the wood grain and shade exactly. Pieces of furniture can be digitally placed into photographs of the room to show the client what to expect, which is critically important as each piece is unique and, in effect, is its own prototype with only one chance to get it absolutely perfect.

Once the client has decided upon and agreed all the specifications of their piece, the technical drawings – or building blueprints – begin. This is all done to exact scale so is rather like building a house in miniature. This process has long been in use: the only difference is that, in earlier times, all plans (technical drawings) were drawn by hand on paper, parchment or tracing paper and so any

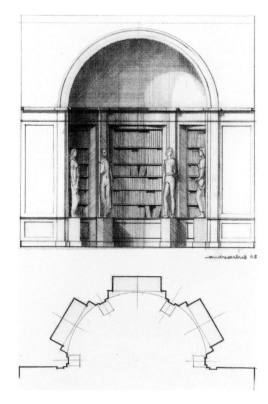

← Library of the Boston Athenaeum, showing a staircase built into the side section of a library to gain access to the gallery.

→ Drawing of 1945 by André Arbus showing sculptures for a library, done for an article by Jean-Charles Moreaux, 'La Sculpture dans l'architecture' in *Art et industrie* (February 1946).

changes had to be 'scratched' out and redrawn which was very time consuming. A specific disadvantage of using tracing paper was its susceptibility to varying humidity, causing it to expand and contract unpredictably and playing havoc with the scale elements.

Not only do digitally constructed technical drawings make it easy to change elements of the design, but in this age of technical overlaying, they also afford the designer the ease of sending furniture layouts digitally to be overmapped by the lighting designer or the M&E (mechanical & engineering) specialist. This saves a great deal of time and makes possible a greater range and complexity of modern design and services.

Cabinet-making in the British workshops used by Gosling has not changed in essence for centuries. Hand-tooling and inlaying; marquetry; turning; sand burning; inlays; and book-matching: these are all techniques and crafts used throughout the generations of

British craftsmanship. Each piece is made by one craftsman only who signs his piece as a matter of pride in his handiwork.

One element of modern craftsmanship that has changed dramatically are the glues. With advances in chemical engineering and the development of synthetics, there is a wide choice of substances for adhering metals and veneers. However, one of the strongest glues in the world (and as expensive as gold) is sturgeon glue, made since Antiquity by boiling down the inner membrane of the sturgeon's air bladder. This glue is still used today in museums such as the Wallace Collection to restore Boulle furniture.

The advent of CAD in designing and redesigning interiors has meant that more is achievable than ever before: The overlaying of different skills is possible, such as quantity surveying, structural engineers, security installation, air conditioning, heating and lighting. All these skills add up to a finished product that is both beautiful and unique.

↑ A hand-drawn sketch by Tim Gosling, with more definition after the initial discussion with the client for a project for a fitted library with a domed apse.

→ Hand sketch by Philip Sturdy at Gosling for a fitted library, showing the relationship of the staircase to the oculus and the apse. Although it was not ultimately possible to put the staircase into an actual bookcase it was possible to hide it behind one of the flanks.

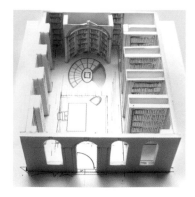

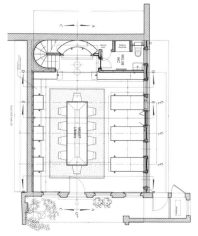

← ← A rough sketch by Tim Gosling drawn during initial discussions with the client for a project for a fitted library with a domed apse, showing a staircase built into the bookcase.

← Problem-solving model of the fitted library design, showing an idea for an oval staircase in front of the apse.

← → Digitally drawn technicals for the library.

↙ The 3-Dimensional Computer Modelling Programme was used to show the ideal design of the library with oculi set evenly around the room to create an optimum rhythm for the eye. Practicality intervened at this stage, when both client and Gosling realised that the rarity of the fifteenth-century reliquaries needed to fill the oculi would stall the project; and thus faced by a choice of vacant oculi, the second option (↘), was approved. The British Museum was consulted on the optimum conditions for keeping rare 16th- and 17th-century books. Interestingly the humidity of England was deemed perfect for them, but they should be kept unheated without direct light and stored flat – hence the lower sections on the left-hand flanks with pull-out shelves.

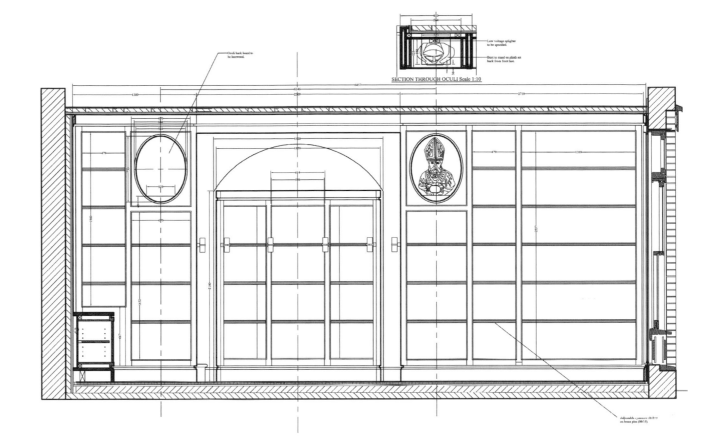

SECTION THROUGH OCULI Scale 1:10

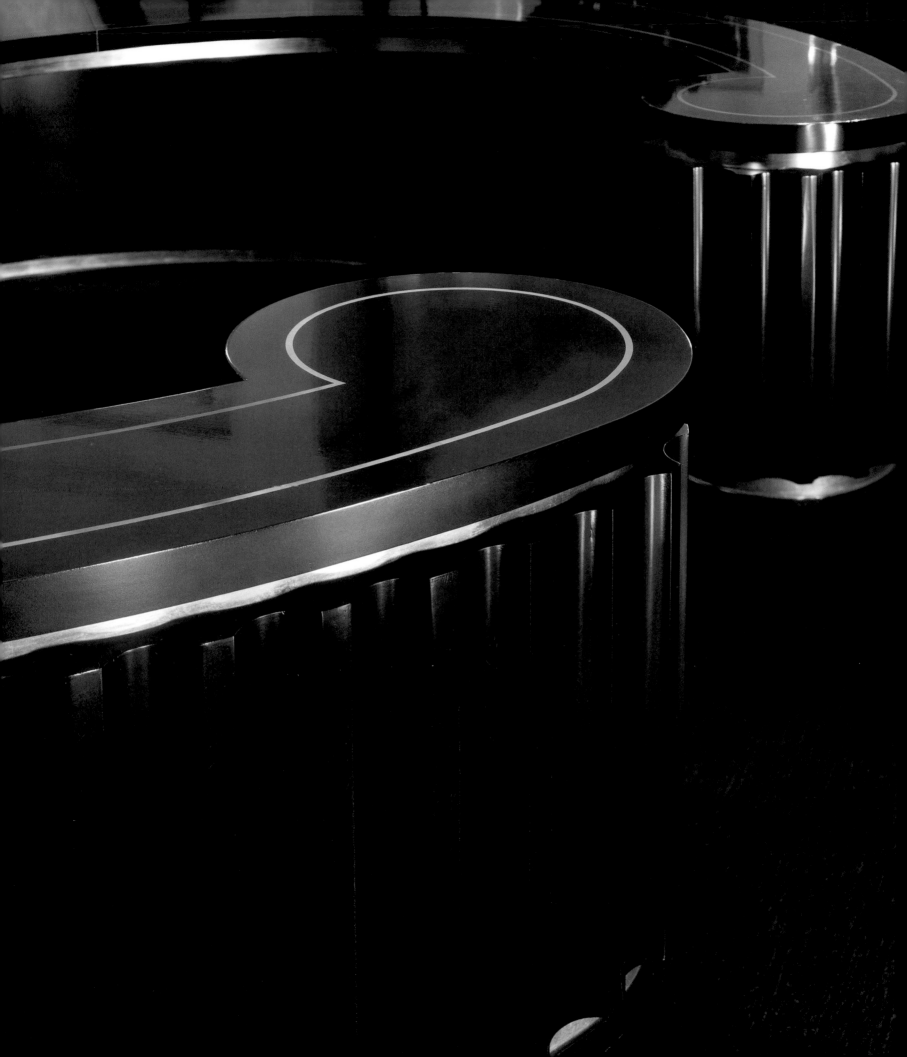

4

The Art and Craft of Luxury

Marquetry

↑ A veneer of amboyna burr, originally from Indonesia – one of the rarest and most expensive woods in the world.

↑ Book matching with marbled Macassar (ebony).

↗ The veneers – in this case English oak – arrive in a drum of cut lengths.

↙ A cut and kiln-dried bundle of burr walnut leaves ready for veneering. Mark Asplin Whiteley Ltd.

At the root of Gosling's craft and expertise is an appreciation and admiration of woods and timbers, the configurations and patterns possible within the grain, and the incredible variety of colours, shades and markings. As a result the technique of veneering has always played a huge part in any Gosling design.

Veneers are very thin sheets or slices of fine-grained, often precious wood, usually between $\frac{1}{16}$" and $\frac{1}{32}$" (1.6 and 0.8 mm) in thickness, applied over a strong support of a less decorative wood or substrate, and are used in furniture, objects and wall panels. The finest and rarest timbers are used for veneers: the bark may be peeled from the tree trunk, or the trunk cut into large rectangular blocks called 'flitches' in order to obtain the veneer. The appearance of the grain comes from slicing through the growth rings of the tree and varies depending upon the angle of cutting.

Veneers are delivered to workshops rolled up in drums and are usually sold by the square foot, but as they can be joined up, even small pieces are used. The production of veneers has the advantage of increasing the amount of usable wood, greatly augmenting the yield of rare woods with interesting grain patterns, thus placing fewer demands on resources.

Veneers can be matched and glued to the surface of the supporting wood to create interesting patterns or beading of fine-grained or coloured wood. Different patterns are obtained by varying the laying of the veneers, the most common of which is book matching, where veneer leaves are alternatively folded out, as in the centre opening of a book, so that one leaf is a mirror image of the other. With slip matching, the leaves are laid face up, side by side, in the order they were found on the original log blocks, so the grain pattern is repeated. Other techniques include reverse slip, radial, diamond or herringbone matching.

Prized veneers include burr veneer ('burl' in the US), caused by pockets of growth in the tree which give a sort of marbling pattern – a very striking 'flame' V-grain of an extremely decorative character, which results from the cut being made at the point where the trunk or heavy branch joins with two forking branches; and swirl veneer which usually appears around knots and crotches, giving a irregular eddying grain.

Parquetry is probably the earliest form of veneering. In the veneer patterns on furniture – as in the block patterns on floors – parquetry uses geometrical pieces of the veneer arranged in different grain directions, cut with a knife or a saw and glued onto a solid wooden base, to form a decorative surface pattern.

← Studiolo from the Ducal Palace in Gubbio, c.1478–82 commissioned by Federico da Montefeltro (1422–1482), Urbino, Italy. Designed by Francesco di Giorgio Martini, executed by Giuliano da Maiano. Walnut, beech, rosewood, oak and fruitwoods in walnut base. The use of the different inlaid woods and techniques create a perspective in which the cupboard doors and shelves are perceived as 3-D, although they are actually physically flat.

↓ Wardrobe, attr. to André-Charles Boulle, c.1700, France. Oak, *première-* and *contre-partie* Boulle marquetry of brass and turtle-shell; the interior of the doors veneered with ebony, purpleheart, and marquetry of ebony, purpleheart and pewter; gilt bronze; steel locks and hinges.

Marquetry is the inlay technique of covering an object with pieces of veneer to form decorative patterns, designs and even entire pictures. The rich palette of colours and patterns that wood provides has resulted in wood veneers long being used as a decorative medium. By the fourteenth century, Italian craftsmen led Europe in the art of marquetry decoration, demonstrating unrivalled skill in the creation of decorative pictorial representations in wood through an inlay technique known as *intarsia*. One of the best known and most spectacular examples is the study commissioned around 1476 by Federico da Montefeltro (1422–1482), Duke of Urbino, still to be seen at the Palace of the Dukes of Montefeltro in Urbino, Italy, with a second example in the Metropolitan Museum, New York.

While highly sophisticated patterns could be produced with early techniques, the ability to cut complex curves was very much limited by the use of the knife as the principal tool. With the developments of skills and techniques a new profession was born: the *marqueteur*. In the seventeenth century the expansion of the European trade routes, especially to the East and West Indies, provided the *marqueteur* with many new and exciting materials. Almost overnight cabinet-makers had access to an extended range of coloured woods in hues of

purple, red, black and yellow. The growth in foreign trade also brought to Europe exotic dyes and stains which could be used to supplement natural wood colours. Brightly coloured floral wood marquetry represented the height of fashion, inspired by the Dutch still-life paintings that were popular at this time. These new materials were endowed with an attractive exoticism and sense of novelty, but their cost was also high, which meant that they could only be used for the most luxurious furniture.

These changing technical possibilities allowed the development of the Boulle marquetry technique, created at the end of the seventeenth century and still in use today. Invented before his birth, it is still André-Charles Boulle (1642–1732) who is generally credited with having further developed this form of marquetry to new heights of refinement in late seventeenth- and early eighteenth-century France, when the craft reached the status of high art. His name lives on today in Boulle work, a technique best known in relation to metals and turtle-shell, although the earliest examples of Boulle marquetry used two contrasting materials such as wood, ivory, bone or turtle-shell.

← Pieces of furniture with rectangular panels are enhanced visually by book matching, as in this Gosling credenza with book-matched walnut veneers. The form of this piece is derived from an antique Chinese chair (seen in the foreground) and the book matching of figured walnut works in harmony with the woods used in the chair.

↑ The use of herringbone veneering is also suited to rectangular or square panels, as used by Gosling in ripple sycamore for a sideboard and wooden door panel.

→ A skillfully executed panel of ripple sycamore in herringbone pattern has visual depth and looks almost three-dimensional.

Circular or D-ended dining
tables are the perfect vehicles
for radial slip matching,
which comes to a point that
fits together twenty-four
lengths of American walnut.
The accuracy and tolerance
of this has to be within half
a millimetre for all ends. The
table-top is bordered by a
cross-banding of ebony.

Parquetry is usually only composed of geometric and repetitive elements and can, like marquetry, be either simple, like this Gosling dining-room cabinet (→ ↓) or highly complex. Technically this dark stained walnut with sycamore parquetry inlay and ebony is exceptionally difficult to achieve, as each section must be sanded so that the ebony does not leach into the white sycamore and discolour it.

The cabinet echoes the design on the entrance of the house – a Regency building in Edinburgh (←). Interior design by Designworks, and architecture by Keppie Design.

A wardrobe in dark stained walnut with ebony parquetry inlay echoes the Greek key design on the cornicing of the bedroom in a Regency house in Edinburgh. The handles are all made in solid ebony with the contrasting interiors in English sycamore.

When using marquetry to depict a scene or picture Gosling have always tried to achieve a sense of realism – using perspective to convey a feeling of depth, as with this colonnade scene inlaid in marquetry on the door of a client's dressing room. This *trompe-l'oeil* effect is achieved not only by using different shades of woods (eight are used in this design: brown oak, English oak, London plane, burr elm, walnut, burr ash, boxwood and sycamore), but also by employing techniques such as sand burning – literally burning the wood with hot sand to scorch it and create a darker hue. The detail in walnut, behind the colonnade on the depiction, is created by sand burning the wood, darkening it to give the illusion of shadow. This colonnade motif is taken from a building in Rome which relates to the Pompeian bathroom behind the door.

Gosling created this table in slip-matched flame mahogany with an ebony edge. The circular dining table expands by splitting in half and adding an extra leaf to become a D-end. The design echoes Regency architecture as shown in the base plinth and the inverted Regency acroteria.

This games table by Gosling is made in walnut with cross-banded rosewood and ebony stringing. The backgammon playing surface is inlaid in satinwood, ripple sycamore and Macassar ebony. The chess pieces and backgammon counters are hand made in sycamore and rosewood, and weighted.

Mirror and Glass

↙ William Orpen, *The Signing of Peace in the Hall of Mirrors, Versailles, 28 June 1919,* 1919. The Imperial War Museum, London.

→ Pier glasses, consoles tables and candelabra in the Saloon of Holkham Hall, Norfolk.

For Gosling the attraction of using glass is its clarity and transparency, which gives an impression of light and air. The mirror's reflective qualities have long been used to amplify the natural and artificial light available in interiors and increase the sense of space. In furniture making in particular, glass is often used in the form of mirror-glass or as a purely decorative, illusionistic element in cabinets and writing desks.

Mirrored surfaces have been used since the Stone Age; the earliest examples were made from highly polished volcanic glass, such as obsidian. Evidence has been found in Anatolia (modern-day Turkey) of polished stone mirrors dating from 6000 BCE, while bronze and copper mirrors dating from between 4000 and 2000 BCE have been found in Mesopotamia, Egypt and China.

Solid, polished metal mirrors, however, were too expensive for widespread use, and their low reflectivity (the reason antique mirrors give a darker reflection than their modern counterparts) made them unsuitable for indoor use, as the artificial lighting of the time was limited to candles and lanterns. The more efficient method of coating glass to create mirrored surfaces has long been used: metal-coated glass dates from about the first century CE, while mirrors backed with gold leaf are mentioned in Roman literature around the same time. The Romans also invented a type of primitive mirror by coating glass with molten lead.

The first manufactured glass, made using sodium carbonate, or soda ash, extracted from vegetation ash, was probably Phoenician; but small glass jars, bottles and beads, including coloured glass created by the addition of different minerals, have been found in Egypt dating from 2000–1500 BCE. There is also evidence that the Egyptians used translucent but very thick window glass from around the first century CE.

The art of glassmaking spread throughout Europe during the time of the Roman Empire, with techniques developing and becoming increasingly sophisticated. This resulted in examples of highly ornate glass designs and the evolution of glass enameling and gilding. An important innovation in glass manufacture occurred in Northern Europe in the eleventh century, with the discovery of how to make glass using potash (potassium carbonate) from the more readily available wood ashes. This formed an important distinction between Northern European glass and that which was made in

the South or Mediterranean regions where soda ash was still used.

The island of Murano – to which the glassmakers' foundries had been relocated by the Venetian Republic in 1291 due to the risk of fire to the city's wooden buildings – had become an extremely important glassmaking centre by the fourteenth century. The Venetian glassmakers had a natural advantage in the abundance of nearly pure silica in the quartz pebbles (*cogoli*) that gathered on the riverbeds of the Ticino and the Adige; and a business advantage in having the sole trade monopoly for the Levant soda ash they used to mix it with. This gave the Venetians superiority over glass producers elsewhere, and Murano glassmakers retained their dominance in glass manufacture for centuries. They developed and refined new, sophisticated techniques in producing luxury materials, such as crystalline glass (*cristallo*); enamelled glass (*smalto*); glass with golden threads shot through (*aventurine*); milk glass (*lattimo*); and the famous multi-coloured glass or *millefiori*.

By the sixteenth century, Venice was also a major centre of mirror manufacture, having invented a way to make mirrors out of ordinary plate glass by coating the back of the glass with a tin–mercury amalgam, thus producing a near perfect reflection and image. Glass mirrors from this period – whether from Venice, the Saint Gobain factory in France, or Bohemia – remained extremely expensive luxury items. Since thin glass is a distinctive characteristic of antique mirrors one way to tell if a mirror is in fact an antique is to hold a coin up to the mirror surface: the closer the reflection is to the coin, the thinner the glass.

Mirror glass in furnishings became popular during the seventeenth century, but the prohibitive cost and difficulty of manufacturing large pieces of mirror restricted both its use in interior design and the possibilities of large-scale application. Mirrors in lavish frames were, however, used as decoration in palaces and courts throughout Europe, with the spectacular Hall of Mirrors at Versailles being a notable example and an outstanding technical achievement for its time (left).

Methods invented by the French glass workshops in the 1700s facilitated fairly large-scale production of mirrors, which led to their relative affordability and prevalence in eighteenth-century interiors. The popularity and wide distribution of mirror glass was stimulated by the need for an increased amount of artificial light. During the sixteenth and seventeenth centuries, this need had been satisfied by placing candles in front of highly polished concave metal plates. But by using silvered mirror glass the light effect was multiplied. Large, silvered wall mirrors, hung over console tables and often placed against pier walls, became a commonplace and functional element, further illuminating interiors lit by artificial light.

Glass and mirrors continue to play an important role in furniture and interior design, although technology has moved on and allows a greater scope and variety of materials – most notably with the invention and subsequent commercial production of acrylic glass in the 1930s. This transparent man-made substrate can be used in place of glass and is on occasion preferable due to the ease of manufacture and low cost.

← Gosling pier glass and table — a contemporary take on the historic arrangement as seen, for example, at Holkham Hall. Interior design by Lyndhurst Interiors.

→ A dining table designed by Gosling with burr walnut pedestals and a clear-glass table-top. Burr (or 'burl') veneer is extremely distinctive, and can transform an item of furniture into a statement piece. As a result it is typically used on panels or surfaces that are on display, and immediately visible. Gosling's most recent use of this remarkable veneer is in this table where the top was constructed in clear glass, allowing an easy view of the striking burr walnut inlaid pedestals beneath (⬎). Interior design by Joanna Trading

↙ A full-size mirrored panel created for an office without external windows, to maximize light and space. The three mirrors echo in life size the windows that look onto this atrium. These were gilded by Peter Binnington and his team and inset with 'antique' mirror. They stand over three metres tall.

→ The antique frames around the room are filled with eglomise to reflect the light and depth of the crystal chandeliers. The frame above has a Pink Panther motif – the Goring Hotel's only acknowledged eglomise thief!

←The shelves of this cabinet are made of glass to allow the light to flow through, and the doors contain panels of timber and acrylic, UV-bonded inlay which allows the internal lighting to shine out, giving the impression of radiance (→). Interior design by Millais Interior Design.

⇒ In the drawing room of Tim Gosling's home this pair of double doors in mahogany were gilded with inset gold leaf with panels of antique mirror glass to reflect back the room. The entire room including double doors are lit by the mahogany border inset into the floor. This creates a dramatic sense of light.

← A mirror placed above a mantel reflects the natural light from a window opposite in Tim Gosling's London home, Sycamore House.

↓ Two full-length antique, 19th-century French mirrors are used to mimic the effect of extra windows by reflecting natural light. These are illuminated with lighting sunk into the carpet beneath them. Bespoke furniture by Gosling. Right-hand circular side table by Nina Campbell.

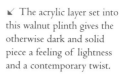

↙ The acrylic layer set into this walnut plinth gives the otherwise dark and solid piece a feeling of lightness and a contemporary twist.

→ An acrylic and dark-stained walnut finial.

In this private home, the acrylic trestle table and acrylic supports designed by Gosling display an eclectic and important collection of Pre-Columbian art, giving the impression that the pieces are floating or hovering.

Vellum

↑ At Rooks Books of
London, sheets of calf
vellum – cleaned, limed and
ready for panel wrapping.

Gosling has revived the use of vellum in its furniture designs, using its exceptional properties to give an aura of glamour, softness and enduring luxury. Vellum is an extremely hard-wearing material traditionally prepared from the fine-grained, unsplit skins of a goat, calf, or sheep which, due to its pale colour and attractive appearance, was used for the writing, painting and gilding of many of the earliest books.

Since the Middle Ages the terms vellum and parchment have become almost interchangeable. There is, however, a definite if subtle difference between the two. Vellum is made from far superior skins to those used for parchment, and some of the processes – particularly the shaving or scraping of the skins to remove skin grain – takes much longer and requires much greater care and skill. By contemporary definition, parchment is prepared from sheep or goat skin whereas vellum (thinner and smoother) is made from the skins of young calves. This, however, is a very modern distinction: historically, animal vellum could be made from the hide of any young mammal, including antelope calves, fawns and even foals, although the latter were generally far too valuable as working animals. Whatever the accepted definitions, vellum has always denoted a higher quality, and a far superior material, than parchment.

Vellum continues to be highly regarded as superlative quality stationery, not only due to its luxurious appearance, but also because of its durability. It owes its long-lasting nature in part to the alkalinizing, 'liming' process it undergoes while being prepared, which neutralizes and protects against the atmospheric nitric and sulphuric acid, largely responsible for the slow decay of papers and leathers. Vellum's worth was championed less than a decade ago in November 1999 when the UK Parliament voted 121 to 53 in favour of maintaining the practice, dating back to 1497, of printing British Acts of Parliament on vellum for archival purposes.

The process of creating vellum today does not differ significantly from that recorded in monastic accounts from the twelfth century. It is the skill of the craftsman that determines the quality, making the difference between a soft, flexible skin and a stiff, brittle one. The sheep, goat and calf skins which arrive at the vellum maker from cattle farmers and abattoirs are carefully sorted through to ensure that they are free from blemishes and scars – an estimated ninety per cent of skins are discarded as unsuitable at this stage. The initial step is to

← Desk by Carlo Bugatti (Italian, 1856–1940) in walnut, copper, pewter and vellum, Italy, c.1902.

→ A commode inlaid with varnished vellum (Parchemin); bronze gilding on the marble top, Paris, c.1740–50.

remove all of the hair with a knife, traditionally moon-shaped to ensure an even pressure all along the blade. The skins then undergo a process to remove the fat and oil with alkalis known as liming, which involves being alternately immersed in clear water and a strong lime solution. This stage can take up to four weeks until the vellum is sufficiently clean and flexible for use.

Although an eggshell or matt surface can be obtained by varying the process, vellums are usually prepared with a semi-shiny grain surface for which the skin is stretched to an even tension and rubbed with pumice to smooth it. The final step is a long-tensioned drying which must be slow and gradual in order to give a flat opaque skin, after which the skins are selected for their commercial requirement according to the type, size, colour, finish and thickness required. Vellum's strength is apparent, with specialist hardware scissors used by craftsmen to cut required sizes from the prepared sheets.

The fundamental difference between vellum and leather is that leather is tanned in acid (an irreversible process), whereas the liming the vellum undergoes is both alkalinizing and reversible, as the lime can be removed in water. Also unlike leather, vellum shows its true surface as the skin is not denatured in any way by the preparation process.

Unsurprisingly, given its hardy but attractive nature, vellum was also used for making luggage, a tradition encouraged by the increase in travel during the nineteenth century and the arrival of the motor car into mainstream society. A recent and interesting exponent of vellum in furniture was Carlo Bugatti (father of the celebrated designer of Bugatti cars, Ettore Bugatti) who began designing furniture around 1880. The first international show of his work was at the Italian Exhibition in London in 1888, where his signature style began to attract admirers, and where he was subsequently awarded an honorary prize. Later in his career the Turkish Salon in New York's Waldorf Astoria was furnished with his pieces — a collection for which he was awarded the Silver Medal at the Paris Exposition Universelle of 1900.

Strikingly original and luxuriantly exotic, Bugatti used vellum to upholster chairs, cover tabletops and inlay desks in his furniture making. Initially he merely inlaid relatively undecorated vellum panels surrounded by decorative borders of metalwork and woods into his pieces; however he soon progressed to covering the entire wooden frame of his furniture with vellum. These pieces were often decorated with stylized patterns and motifs hand-painted directly onto the vellum with gold leaf and watercolours or dye.

One interesting example is a writing desk designed by Bugatti. The writing surface is covered in vellum, held in place with punched copper strapping and the walnut legs inlaid with pewter, imitating calligraphic brush painting. The unusual profile of the desk suggests the jaws and teeth of an alligator. This desk was part of one of Bugatti's few completed interiors: a bedroom designed for the London residence of Lord Battersea.

DESIGN FOR A WONDOROUS BOX for SIR HANS SLOANE

Gosling has always believed that great design requires the designer to push through boundaries and preconceptions; mixing styles, techniques and genres to create something unique. It was with this in mind that Gosling approached two very different projects, blending the ancient with the modern. In the first example Gosling, in collaboration with Rooks Books of London, began to experiment with new techniques enabling drawings to be 'printed' onto vellum using a laser printer with archival inks. The printed skins are then lacquered and can be wrapped around panels to create unique pieces such as the lid designed for a box. The engraving is a 1772 elevation by Robert Adam of the south courtyard wall in the home of Sir Watkin Williams Wynn, Baronet, in St James's Square. The Gosling sketch (←) shows the design to be wrapped around the outside of the box. The predecessor to this modern technique was embossing gold foil on vellum as in this bookbinding of *An Artist in Italy* (↓).

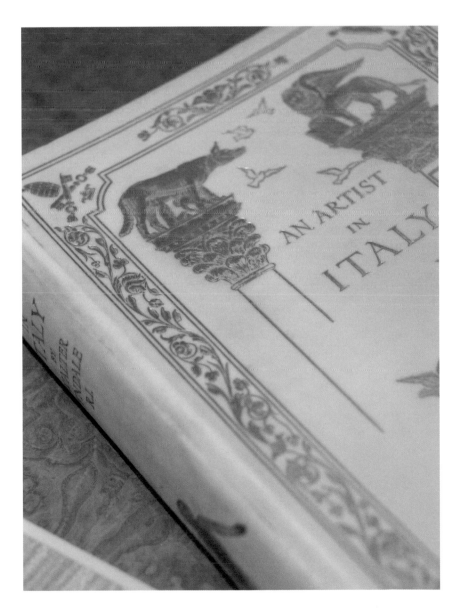

←← ↓ In the second instance, Gosling created a TV cabinet with doors of individually vellum-wrapped panels, glued and set into ripple sycamore and set into a walnut frame. The effect is such that the ripple sycamore on the door interiors mimic the feel and look of the vellum inlaid on the exterior. While the colour of vellum is unaffected by sunlight, over time ripple sycamore, if exposed, would darken into honey tones – however being on the inside of the cabinet means the doors will retain their tonal balance (→). The cabinet also has full cable management to allow complete concealment of any unsightly wires.

→→ A private client commissioned Gosling to create a feature out of an imposing floor-to-ceiling bank of wardrobes in their central London home. In order to 'tone down' the ceiling-height doors, Gosling rebuilt them with individual vellum-wrapped panels, glued and hand-wrapped onto sycamore, and set into a sycamore frame. The design made a decorative feature of an otherwise functional element of the room, avoiding any visual imbalance and creating an environment of warmth and tactility.

Shagreen

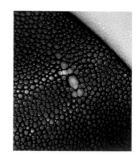

⬊ Shagreen hides in a
Gosling workshop. Shagreen
hides can be dyed in the
same manner as leather
to suit the client's
requirements (⬆).

The story of shagreen (Fr. *galuchat*) is an eventful one. This tactile, granular hide, fashioned from the skins of sharks and stingrays, has been prized by craftsmen for its beauty and durability from ancient times, and has alternately enjoyed huge popularity in the world of design, or fallen into disuse and disappeared for centuries.

Shagreen is extremely durable, its rough surface made up of small, round, closely set 'beads' which vary in size depending on the size and age of the animal. The treatment of these beads divides shagreen into the two distinct categories of unshaved and shaved shagreen. Unshaved shagreen hides have, as the name suggests, not been sanded down at all so the characteristic, round beads are full and rough to the touch. Their waxen surface means that any dye used to treat the skin does not soak into the hide, but rather sits on top, giving it a strikingly glossy appearance. Shaved shagreen hides, on the other hand, are much smoother to the touch, with the beads sanded down quite extensively. This allows the dye to permeate all the way through the hides resulting in a more subtle, matt colour. The granulated surface is often created artificially, by stamping, on the untanned skins of horses and mules to imitate shagreen.

Early Japanese and Mayan civilisations believed that the stingray gave power and strength to those who handled it, and its spine was considered to bring protection, luck and prosperity. When using shagreen in furniture the spine is often a design feature and can almost be book-matched, as with timber. The spine, being slightly raised, gives the piece character, extra tactility and rhythm – as well as identifying it as authentic ray skin – as shown on p. 104, inlaid into a panel of a gentleman's pedestal desk constructed in American black walnut and Santos rosewood with brushed nickel stringing and beading.

Armour and a number of ornamental items inlaid with shagreen have been found in the tombs of the Egyptian pharaohs. There is also evidence of shagreen being used during the Han dynasty (206 BCE–220 CE) in China, as well as in eighth-century Japan where it was used as an inlay on the sheath handles of Samurai swords and daggers, its rough surface improving the warrior's grip on the battlefield.

By the seventeenth century shagreen was being used as an inlay in furniture and for small articles such as cases, and in book-binding and pocket books. However its great revival came in the mid-eighteenth century thanks to Jean-Claude Galluchat, a master leatherworker in the

← Mark of John Paul Cooper, Toilet service, London, 1925–29. Cooper described shagreen as 'a material possessing some of the qualities of both mother-of-pearl and leather. Its little nodules of concentric rings give one, when the skin is particularly translucent, the feeling of looking deep down into a pool of sea-green water'.

◢ André Groult, Anthropomorphic chiffonier in mahogany wrapped in shagreen, ivory and silvered handles, c.1925, France.

court of Louis XV of France. It quickly became fashionable amongst the French aristocracy and by the 1750s its use had spread throughout Europe. From this time on it became usual to see shagreen in pieces dyed pale green, giving a subtle, natural and luxurious finish. In practice shagreen can be dyed any number of colours, especially in today's workshops.

At the very end of the nineteenth century the English artisan John Paul Cooper (1869–1933) took the art of shagreen to new heights. Often staining, polishing and mounting it in silver, he used it mainly to decorate boxes but also a number of vases, candlesticks, picture- and mirror-frames.

Thereafter shagreen fell out of favour almost completely until the 1920s when it caught the public's eye once more, reaching its peak of popularity in the 1930s and 1940s. Shagreen was soon being used by eminent Art Deco designers Émile-Jacques Ruhlmann, Jean-Michel Frank, Clément Rousseau, André Groult and André Arbus as elements of marquetry, as well as wrappings over the curved edges of tables and cabinets, a technique for which shagreen, with its softness and malleability, is particularly suited.

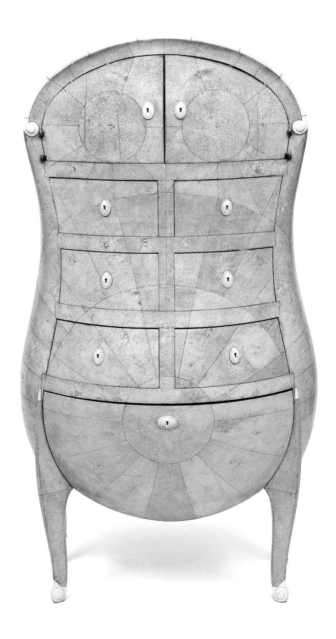

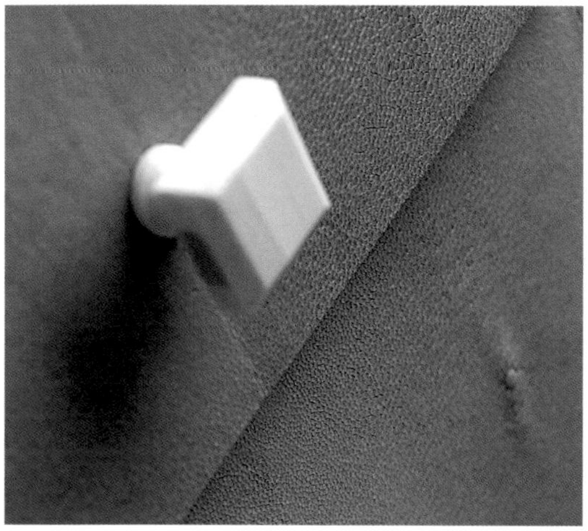

↖ The spine of the stingray in shagreen is used to cover or wrap a Gosling chest of drawers with faux bone handles and turned sycamore feet, designed in the 1940s style.

↑→ The textured, almost iridescent surface of shagreen inlaid into the top of a ladies' dressing table.

→ Bedroom in a Nash-designed London house on Regent's Park with Gosling furniture inspired by the quoining on the front terrace, and using a grey shagreen to harmonise with the silks and suede chosen for this room. Interior design by Bill Bennette Design.

Shagreen inlaid into the surface of a 1940s André Arbus-inspired dressing table/writing desk in cream lacquer, with brass detailing and shagreen-inlaid top supported by eight turned and tapered legs with brass feet. The eye of the stingray spine in the shaved and dyed shagreen can be clearly seen (←). Interior design by Alidad.

↓→ The spine of the stingray in shagreen inlaid into a panel on the top of a gentleman's pedestal desk. The front and rear elevations of the desk also sport four rectangular inlaid panels of shagreen, surrounded by a beading of sterling silver. The main desk is in rosewood.

↖ A pair of bedside tables in myrtle burr with unshaved shagreen in a caramel colour. The eye of the shagreen is more rounded and textured as it is unsanded.

←→ Gosling, with Joanna Trading, created this desk in cherry with the top book-matched in white shaved shagreen.

⇒ This shagreen bar by Gosling in facetted chocolate brown lacquer supports a radial shagreen top beneath a Tracey Emin neon sculpture, and is positioned opposite a French carved marble fireplace.

↓ Chair with stamped leather covers. Maker unknown, Portugal, c.1720–40. Carved and turned walnut with embossed and incised leather back and seat trimmed with brass-covered pine domes (simulating nail-heads); oak seat rails and pine back-frame. Unidentified arms and crest in embossed leather back-cover.

leather; and drying and staking to soften the leather by passing it over a series of blunt pins that pummel and flex it. The leather is then finished by buffing, with the application of coatings to the surface of the leather to protect it and make it easier to maintain, improve its water resistance and durability and to enhance its colour and appearance.

Because of its durability and comfort, leather has been used for seating purposes throughout the history of transportation (including for the hulls of early boats). In furniture, in addition to its use in seating and the upholstery of chairs and couches, leather was also used in interiors to cover chests, tables and desks – particularly on the working or writing surfaces.

Leather was also used in a decorative fashion for wall panels and stamped leather upholstery, often painted or gilded and embossed in a style originating from twelfth-century North Africa, which was introduced to Portugal and Spain and is sometimes therefore referred to as 'Spanish leather'. The technique reached Flanders and Brabant in the Low Countries around the end of the fifteenth century. By the seventeenth century this technique was being used for chair covers – backs and seats – and as writing tables and bed-backs by the eighteenth century. Examples of

the rich and ornamented leather wall panels can be seen today at the National Trust properties of Dyrham Park in Gloucestershire and Ham House in London, where they are stretched on battens like damask wall-hangings.

Embossing leather is still common today, but is a process used increasingly to imitate exotic and rare skins, such as crocodile or python, as demanded by the luxury goods market. The imitation of cowhide by embossing, stamping and colouring has in fact become widely accepted, both for reasons of expense and to protect the species endangered by the trend. The skill involved in this is so extraordinary, and the resulting skins so versatile that it is sometimes difficult to tell the difference between a real exotic skin, or a stamped leather one. Skins from ostrich, kangaroo, seal, crocodile, alligator, lizard, snakes, and shagreen (see p. 96) are, however, still occasionally used in furniture making or upholstery.

The fashion for upholstered chairs and sofas – a very European and Anglo-Saxon phenomenon – gradually increased the use of leather in interiors, particularly as gentlemen's clubs flourished, and contributed to its popularity, resulting in heavily stuffed forms, including the widely adopted Chesterfield sofa.

Leather's pliancy and versatility make it a perfect material to 'wrap' around furniture to great effect. One such example is this matching set of bedside tables and a dressing table by Gosling. Constructed in dark stained walnut, with ebony inlays, the pieces are then wrapped in a thick chocolate-brown leather with a finishing edge of solid ebony.

The leather wrapping is mitred onto the corner detail to take the eye into the drawer fronts made of dark stained walnut and ebony. The handles are porcelain bone. Interior design by Designworks with architecture by Keppie Design.

Lacquer

↑ René Dubois,
The Dubois Commode,
Paris, c.1765. Oak veneered
commode with Japanese
lacquer, black stained
purplewood and mahogany
(on the legs); gilt bronze;
a brecciated Sarrancolin
marble top; silk, paper and
gimp (lining drawers).

The art of lacquer work has a long and colourful history, with its genesis in China, Japan, and South-East Asia. The term 'lacquer' can be applied to many different substances, and cover a variety of techniques. 'True lacquer' or 'oriental lacquer' is often used to refer to artwork made from, or covered with, resin extracted from the *urushi sumac* group of trees: *Urushi-no-ki* or *Rhus verniciflua* Stokes in Japan, China and Korea; Annan *urushi* or *Rhus succedanea L.* in Vietnam and Taiwan; and *Melanorrhoea laccifer* (black tree) in Burma and Thailand. There are three main types of wood-decorated Chinese lacquer: low relief, surface-painted and incised. During the great period of Chinese carved lacquer in the fourteenth and fifteenth centuries, between one hundred and two hundred layers could be built up to gain the depth of reflection sought.

The European fascination with rare and exotic objects from China and the Far East began in the first half of the seventeenth century, a fashion which continued unabated throughout the eighteenth and nineteenth centuries. In response to this demand, a new style of export lacquer evolved during the 1630s – pieces of superlative craftsmanship and quality, with characteristics more similar to

domestic lacquer than the previous export standard. One such piece is the Mazarin Chest, one of the finest pieces of Japanese export lacquer to have survived, decorated with scenes from the *Tale of Genji* and the *Tale of the Soga Brothers*. It is assumed that, like other examples of export lacquer, the Mazarin Chest was either shipped directly to Europe or to an official of the Dutch East India Company serving in the Dutch East Indies.

While the development of the shipping industry and the expansion of maritime trade routes meant lacquer work could be imported into Europe in reasonable quantities, it was still both expensive and insufficient for the demand. The high cost and dearth of lacquer imports led European designers and craftsmen to create imitation lacquered pieces using new and different techniques – a trend fuelled by the restrictions which closed Japan to Western trade in the late seventeenth century. French lacquered furniture was generally considered to be superior in design and execution to the Dutch or English equivalents, but it was Italian lacquer work, particularly from Venice, that was most highly regarded.

One European technique was japanning, which involved the application of several coats of varnish onto a resin base, each layer heat-

→ The Mazarin Chest, Kyoto, Japan, c.1640. Black lacquered wood with gold and silver *hiramaki-e* and *takamaki-e* lacquer, detailing in gold, silver and *shibuichi*, border inlaid with shell and gilded *shakudo* fittings. Victoria and Albert Museum, London. Museum no. 412:1-1882 H 59 × W 101.5 × D 63.9 (cm)

dried and polished. A huge array of interiors, furniture and objects were finished using these methods: from lacquered rooms through to clocks, cabinets and commodes; from tables, bureaux and day-beds to small objects such as mirrors, inkstands and snuff boxes. Layer upon layer of pigmented varnish, often in gold on black or red, re-created the striking effect of genuine Asian lacquer.

French polishing is a form of lacquering using the refined, scarlet, resinous secretion of the lac beetle (*Laccifer lacca*), known as shellac. This was used for thousands of years in Assam, India and China as a pigment or dye before its properties as a coating material were discovered. Arriving in Europe via the Silk Road, it is still one of the main ingredients for japanning on wooden objects, and today comes from managed forests in India and Asia.

Vernis Martin lacquer is a transparent lacquer created in the early eighteenth century by four brothers, Guillaume, Simon-Etienne, Julien and Robert Martin. They perfected recipes and applications of varnishes imitating *urushi* lacquer and in 1730 were granted a monopoly by Louis XIV, which was renewed, for making '*toutes sortes d'ouvrages en relief de la Chine et du Japon*'. This lacquer work became all the rage in Paris, and is often cited as being the best oriental lacquer substitute available in the eighteenth century.

J. Watin, a contemporary of the Martin brothers, gives the recipe of Vernis Martin as an oleoresinous (oil-resin) lacquer made by dissolving either fresh tree resin, such as rosin or colophony, mastic or dammar, or a fossilized resin, such as amber, in an oil using quite complex techniques. However in reality the Martin brothers produced many different colours and finishes, in three different workshops for around fifty years, so we can be certain that not only applications but also recipes varied.

Despite the inventiveness of local craftsmen, oriental lacquer work was so much sought after in Europe during the seventeenth and eighteenth centuries that it was commonplace to strip lacquer work from its original piece, re-veneer it onto contemporary furniture and then further embellish it with gilt-bronze. This is beautifully illustrated by the Dubois Commode in the Wallace Collection, London. In the nineteenth century the expanding commercial lacquer production in Europe resulted in a decline in quality.

In the early twentieth century nitrocellulose lacquer was developed. This had the advantage of being able to provide a relatively durable exterior finish combined with quick drying-time. The development of the spray gun made this synthetic polymer hugely popular in furniture manufacture, as well as in the car industry, however major drawbacks include high toxicity and high flammability, even years after application. Since then other lacquers were developed include variations of acrylics, which are also synthetic polymers, some of which are water based like many household paints and glues; and others which are two-part reaction materials such as two-part epoxy resins. There are also solvent-free paints and many other specialised coating materials available today. Much research has been carried out into old paint recipes and many modern paints are based on these, such as emulsion paints, i.e. water and oil. Today natural resins, oils or waxes are further processed in new combinations. In Japan, for example, many of the toxic enzymes have been removed from *urushi*, making the material more user-friendly but also changing the properties of this material.

Gosling designs lacquer furniture for both contemporary domestic and corporate interiors. The preparation of each piece continues to require great skill and attention, and the techniques closely follow the traditional methods. Multiple layers of lacquer are sprayed onto perfectly prepared surfaces in very thin and even layers to ensure that it dries to a hard, glossy finish with great depth and luminosity. The skill involved in getting each layer completely flat and even is tremendous, as in this drinks cabinet constructed in black lacquered sycamore, with a sycamore interior. A visual edge top and bottom is created by masking off the lacquerwork to allow the base sycamore to show through.

← These Gosling bookcases in black lacquer with fillets of gold leaf place the lights in the section of the case. The dining table is inlaid with silver leaf and gold bosses. Interior design by Anouska Hempel Design.

↓ A bookcase in black lacquer with gilded inlay – designed as one of four to stand in front of the boardroom windows. Due to Grade I listed building consent it was not possible to permanently fix the bookcases to the floor, so these stand on lacquered steel stepped plates.

← ↑ → In this design for a corporate client, each piece displays giltwork detailing – an effect created in the same way as the burnished, water-gilding effect shown on the Mazarin Chest (see p. 117), and inlays of brass in the top sections.

⇒ A croissant-shaped lacquer reception desk with brass inlay by Gosling. The strength of the lacquering and fluting holds its own against the double-height onyx staircase of the entrance hall. Interior design by Anouska Hempel Design.

Gilding

→ The last remaining supplies of English beaten-gold leaf, with a gilder's tip; a traditional gilder's cushion with side sections in vellum (old vellum documents are traditionally used for this); applying the gold leaf in the oil-gilding technique with a gilder's tip; Peter Binnington applying the gold leaf.

↙ Flattening down the gold leaf.

Gold has always had an almost mystical allure, capturing the imagination and bestowing a sense of grandeur and richness on the furniture and interiors it adorns. Over the centuries its popularity and demand have never noticeably waned. Like many others Gosling maintain an enduring fascination with this precious metal, and their work with gilders has helped the art of gilding to survive and develop.

Gilding is the art of applying a thin layer of metal to an object or surface. While any metal can be applied using the technique, including silver, palladium, aluminium and copper alloys, gold is by far the preferred material due to its lustre and non-tarnishing properties.

The Egyptians used gold leaf and gold wire three thousand years ago, and they experimented with different alloys of gold and other metals to achieve varying shades in their gilding. A striking example of Egyptian gilded furniture is the throne of Tutankhamun discovered in the antechamber of his tomb.

The age of Roman luxury, generally agreed to have begun after the sacking of Carthage in 146 BCE, was heralded by the gilding of the interior timber ceilings of temples and palaces including the Capitol. The gold used in ancient Rome was applied so thickly that the traces remaining today retain their brilliance and solidity.

By the first century BCE mercury gilding of bronze and copper had also been mastered, as Vitruvius mentions. Early examples of gilding show that the gold was applied to a gesso base prepared by mixing chalk or marble dust with animal glue.

Over the centuries gilding has been used commonly as the most sumptuous of decorative arts on picture- or mirror-frames and furniture, in both religious and secular arts as well as throughout architecture. Experimentation and research has led to differing shades, textures and lustres of gilding being developed and perfected; and these artistic and scientific techniques have led to its application to a wide variety of surfaces.

Gold is an extremely soft and malleable material which means it can be worked into wire or sheets of only a few hundred atoms in diameter. It can be hammered by hand, while cold, into thin sheets – one hundred thousand leaves will be only 1.5 cm thick. One troy ounce of 31.1 g (not even the weight of most chocolate bars) can be beaten into gold leaf to cover 9 m².

The basic techniques of gilding have changed little since the earliest times. Although certain basic procedures apply to all types of

gilding – for example very careful preparation of the ground to be gilded – there is a very wide range of methods and materials used, depending on the nature of the support and the type of object being gilded.

The main types of gilding used in architectural or furniture decoration are oil or mordant gilding and water gilding, along with fire or mercury gilding and electroplating for smaller, decorative elements which are then fixed to the furniture.

Water gilding gives an extremely refined and elegant finish and is used mainly for fine objects such as frames, furniture, sculpture, fine art and religious artifacts; but also for the decoration of stately buildings. Firstly a gesso, a base made of chalk or gypsum mixed with a size (an animal glue, usually from rabbit skin), is applied to the surface to be gilded. This is followed by a thin size wash, often coloured with ochre, and then by the clay-like substance, bole. Glair (adhesive made from egg-white) may also be used as an alternative method of glazing. This is much more fragile and tends to 'craze', or develop a fine network of cracks, over time. Different shades of bole give varying lustres as the gold leaf is so thin that the colour of the bole will affect the appearance, particularly in the case of burnished gilt work.

Water and a tiny amount of size, mixed with alcohol (usually gin) to break down the surface tension, is applied to the dried bole in small areas at a time. This sticks the loose gold leaf used in water gilding to the surface.

Each leaf has to be picked up with a gilder's tip and applied with great care; a wetting brush or mop is used to wet the bole with the size water and, through capillary action, the loose gold leaf is pulled onto the surface. This type of gilding is probably the most rewarding and most time-consuming technique used today by individual craftsman. However it is also one of the most fragile types of gilding; the use of clay, chalk and gypsum, which are hydroscopic and water-soluble, mixed with an animal protein, make it vulnerable to water and moisture damage.

Burnishing is a technique used to achieve a high lustre by rubbing the applied gold leaf with a tool tipped by a polished agate stone. These tools, or burnishers, come in many different sizes and angles for specialized work. Water gilding is universally considered the most superior of all methods as it allows for more variety and a far higher lustre in the finish. Eighteenth-century French gilders were able to burnish a frame to varying degrees in different places, depending on the lighting in the room it

↓ Throne made of wood
overlaid with gold leaf from
the tomb of Tutankhamun,
Valley of the Kings, Dynasty
XVIII, c.1352 BCE.

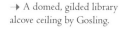

→ A domed, gilded library
alcove ceiling by Gosling.

⇢ Gilded cornice and
ceiling in the Goring Hotel
Lounge by Gosling. The
domed ceiling sections and
the original cornicing are
hand gilded and distressed,
with a deep red bole visible
in glimpses. The gilding was
created by DKT.

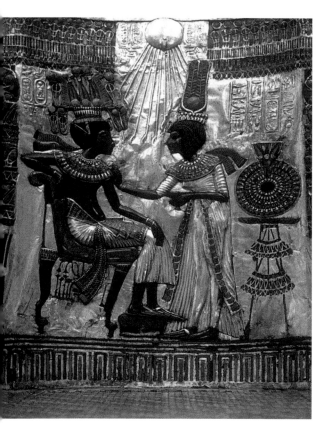

was intended for, so it caught and reflected the light evenly, thus balancing the reflectiveness.

Oil gilding is the simplest form and is mainly used for decorative architectural details, fixed furnishings and exterior work. However there are plenty of cases where it is used for furniture, and in particular picture frames and mirrors, but as oil gilding cannot be burnished it can never achieve the shine or depth of water gilding.

To carry out oil gilding the surface has to be both dry and non-porous and, depending on what result is desired, the oil size may be applied over a coloured base. This oil size (usually linseed oil) will have a known drying time – a time window in which it stays tacky so the gold, as either leaf or transfer gold (fixed onto paper), can be applied to the surface. As with water gilding, the colour beneath the oil size will show through the gold leaf and a

combination of oil and water gilding on one object is quite common to give the object more definition.

Fire gilding or mercury gilding can only be applied on specific, well-prepared metals or alloys and is a highly toxic process. The most common examples of this method in furniture are the gilt-bronze mounts which are used as decorative items on furniture particularly in the eighteenth and nineteenth centuries (see p.161).

Electroplating involves gold, dissolved in an aqueous solution, being deposited onto another conductive object using an electric current. The thickness of gold deposited onto the surface can be controlled with the electric current and with the exposure time. This process, invented in the early nineteenth century, became an industrialised process within several decades and is today used on many everyday items.

The carving, gilding and finished result of a water-gilded and burnished frame for a mirror by Gosling.
↑ At Carvers and Gilders, hand sketching the carving in life size gives an idea of the 'weight' and 'feeling' of the carving and design. ↗ The different gold leaf types – including platinum and silver leaf. Sculpting the fullness of the top urn in the mirror. Water gilding with a gilder's tip.

→ The finished gilded mirror.

←→ Detail of the frame. The client particularly wanted to create her favourite flower in carved and gilded lime. This shows the three-dimensional design of lily-of-the-valley. Interior design by Millais Interior Design.

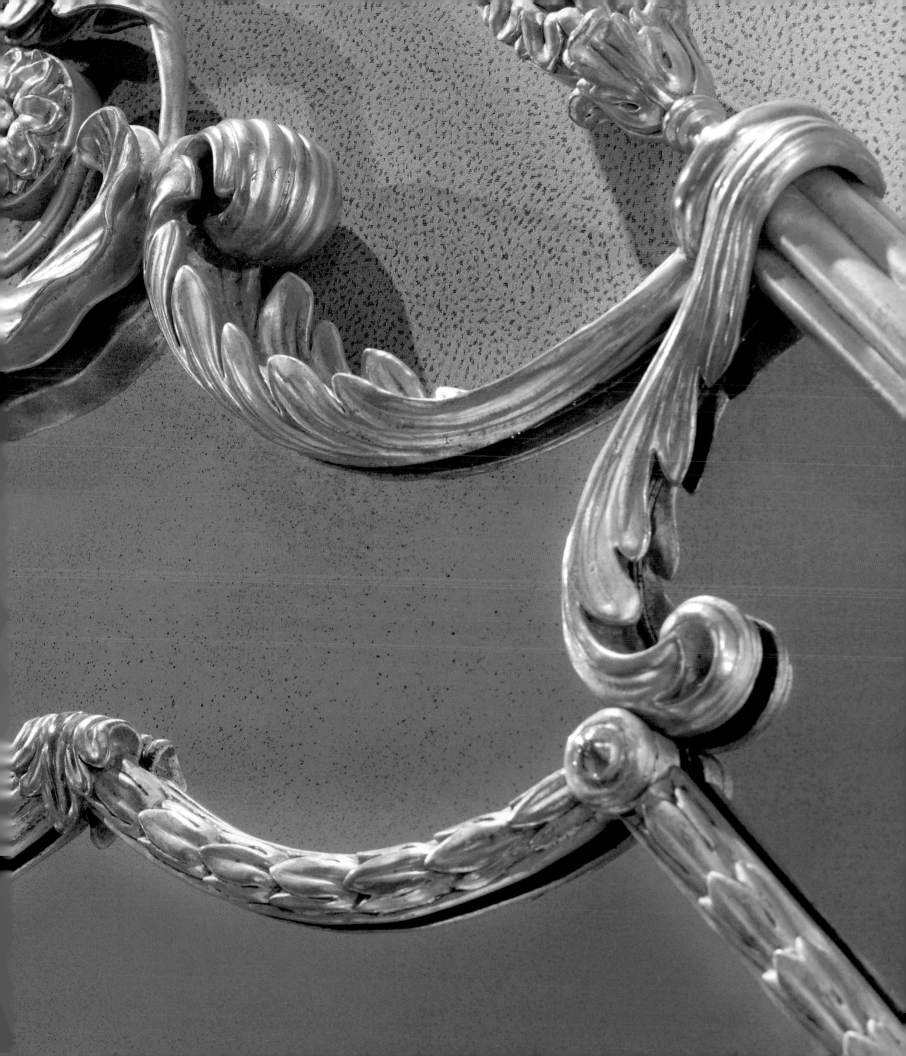

← A pair of three-metre-tall water-gilded and burnished eglomise mirrors based on the exact elevation of the window opposite. The room was wrapped in black silk to offer a dramatic contrast with the gilding. The carpet was hand made in contrasting gold and black silk to echo the band of gilding in the double reception desks. These in turn reflect the fluting of the columns which support the double apse. Interior design by Anouska Hempel Design.

→ Georgian gilded cornicing in Sycamore House, Tim Gosling's London home. The Parthenon Frieze, hand-gilded and painted in grisaille, wraps around the room.

Eglomise

↙ Attributed to René and Thomas Pelletier, A mirror with *verre églomisé* border, London, England, *c*.1707. A full length, cast glass, mirror with borders of *verre églomisé* and silvered pinewood. The ornamental pattern used here is close to the engravings of Jean Bérain (d.1711), court designer to Louis XIV (r.1643–1715). The figures in the lower borders represent Flora, the classical goddess of flowers, and her husband Zephyr, the west wind of springtime.

→ A late Roman/Early Christian *verre églomisé* medallion showing a married couple with Christ. Probably from the catacombs, Rome, 4th century CE. A gold-glass 'medallion' bearing the busts of a man and woman are encircled by a plain border and the inscription 'DULCIS ANIMA VIVAS' ('Sweetheart, may you live [long]'). The medallion would have originally decorated the base of bowl made as a wedding present. Between the two figures a youthful man (Christ) dressed in a cloak and tunic holds wreaths over their heads.

The technique of *verre églomisé* (or eglomise from Fr. 'gilded glass') has not varied greatly over the centuries, and it continues to be a very time-consuming and highly skilled process. There remain a few craftsmen working in the United Kingdom who are capable of carrying out this magical process at the level of excellence required for bespoke interiors, and Gosling has worked closely with such craftsmen to keep this fascinating and magical technique alive.

Verre églomisé is a process where the reverse side of a piece of glass is gilded with gold, silver or metal leaf, and sanded down; often a design is then etched into this base. A coloured background (or bole) can also be painted over the back of the panel, showing through the etching to various degrees and giving the eglomise a distressed appearance.

The origin of the name is generally attributed to Jean-Baptiste Glomy, an eighteenth-century French frame maker to Louis XVI, who used the technique extensively to decorate mirrors for Marie-Antoinette. Dealers began to refer to such work as being 'Glomyised', (Fr. '*églomisé*'). However, there is still some controversy over this theory.

Although the finest examples of eglomise work were carried out in the seventeenth and eighteenth centuries (for example the tearooms of the Caffè Florian in St Mark's Square in Venice) the technique of decorating glass with engraved gold leaf dates back to pre-Roman times. The earliest known examples of *verre églomisé* were found on two bowls from a tomb at Canosa, in Italy, dating from the third century BCE, and displayed today in the British Museum. The Romans developed a method of fixing the gold between two layers of glass in order to protect the delicate leaf; the edges of the bowls were then sealed, with no visible joins, resulting in what is known as 'sandwich glass'. Other examples of *verre églomisé* from the third and fourth centuries are to be found on medallions cemented into Roman burial chambers, where the motifs in gold leaf upon the glass included both Jewish and Christian symbols, together with portraits and inscriptions.

Verre églomisé is extremely labour intensive and requires great skill, so as a result its popularity has waxed and waned over the centuries. From the late fifteenth century to the early eighteenth century the most impressive examples came from European workshops, with many splendid pieces being made in Roman Augsburg (in modern-day Germany) where *verre églomisé* had been popular since medieval times.

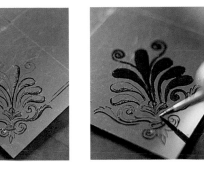

← A pattern is etched onto the back of the silver leaf using a bone or ivory scraper; a deep red bole is then applied to the pattern – it will show through where the silver leaf has been etched.

→ In Peter Binnington's studio silver leaf is placed on the gelatin size applied to a sheet of glass.

During the seventeenth century, shellac became a common material used as a background for *verre églomisé*, as the translucency of shellac was enhanced by overlaying silver leaf, adding more luminosity and depth. Eglomise also began to be used extensively on mirrors, and inset into pieces of furniture and other decorative items in the form of panels.

The Queen Anne period (1665–1714) was one of the most prolific for engravers and gilders. As a result of the dearth of mirrors before the 1690s – almost certainly resulting from the expense of foreign mirrors – the Duke of Buckingham started a glassworks in Vauxhall in 1662, but its skill was limited. By the end of the seventeenth century, however, other factories had emerged and the quality of production had improved. Larger, better quality mirrors became available and pier glasses, which filled the space between windows, became popular. *Verre églomisé* was frequently used as decoration on mirrors during this time. One theory suggests that, given the standard of the draughtsmanship displayed, and the delicacy and range of line engraving, the gold leaf was in fact being etched by highly skilled steel engravers.

The popularity of *verre églomisé* was at its height in France by the late eighteenth century, with exquisite paintings characterized by opulent gilt ornamentation being shipped around the world. In Europe, thousands of churches and chapels in Germany, Austria, Romania and Czechoslovakia, as well as Spain, Portugal and Italy, provided a constant demand for reproduction paintings, and eglomise provided a beautiful and appropriately ornate method of framing these pictures.

The fashion for *verre églomisé* spread to the New World toward the end of the eighteenth century, where it was centred around Baltimore. Furniture, mirror-frames and wall clocks incorporating eglomise panels were produced, for example the 1800 American Federal-style mirrors where the columns on either side are bridged by a frieze of *verre églomisé* panels.

The next period of vogue for *verre églomisé* came during the 1920s and 1930s. Furniture designers incorporated panels into tables, cabinets and cupboards where the shimmering, luxurious surfaces provided an elegant complement to Art Deco interiors. By the mid-twentieth century eglomise painting once more faded into obscurity, but in recent years more awareness of the discipline exists and it is beginning again to find favour in sophisticated interior decors on table-tops, mirrors, and wall coverings, or is integrated into other elements of furniture such as libraries.

In modern workshops little in the eglomise process has changed since the techniques of the fifteenth century. The first step of the process involves a glue or size made from gelatine and water, which is applied to a sheet of glass; this is then followed by the gold or silver leaf. At this stage, before the size dries, the craftsman is able to move the metallic leaf around and place it exactly. Once correctly placed, the back of the glass is then dried relatively quickly using a stream of hot air, after which the leaf adheres tightly, taut and burnished, onto the glass, giving a mirror-like reflective finish.

At this stage the metallic leaf can be sanded down, using a pumice stone, until it is translucent on the surface of the glass, and a pattern can be traced or etched, in reverse through it, using a sharpened bone or ivory scraper. As the fifteenth century handbooks describe, this must be done with painstaking care as it can never be erased or corrected. A coloured bole is then be applied to this reverse side, so it shows through where the foil leaf has been scraped away, resulting in glimpses of colour in contrast to the shine of the silver.

←—→ A panel of *verre églomisé* by Gosling, backed by a red bole, reflecting the chandeliers above. This panel of *verre églomisé* is inset onto the surface of a low table in the Goring Hotel Lounge. The silver leaf eglomise has been lightly sanded and had a red bole applied that shows through the silver leaf in varying degrees, to echo the red silk on the walls by Pierre Frey and the red bole used in the gilded ceiling.

←→ A full-length mirror by Gosling, made up of *verre églomisé*. The silk fabric on the walls is by Pierre Frey and was used as it resembles the braiding on military jackets to evoke a sense of Empire style.

⟶⟶ *Verre églomisé* library with full-height uprights of eglomise set behind the walnut columns. These are in silver leaf with an underbole of dark, slate blue. The double doors are made from *verre églomisé* with a light red bole background to bring out the warmth of the walnut library.

Antique *verre églomisé* panels reflect a pair of walnut cabinets and expanding dining table by Gosling. The painting above the fireplace is *The Three Graces* by Jonathon Coleman.

Inlays

◤ André-Charles Boulle (attr.), Cabinet on a stand, France, c.1665–70, (gilt bronzes by Jacques Caffiéri). In carving these patterns out, Boulle created a 'negative' of the original, where the tortoise shell now formed the background and the brass the pattern – this gave rise to the two processes which bear his name – *Boulle* and *Counterboulle*. Boulle placed gold leaf and other materials under the tortoise shell, chased the brasswork with a graver (engraving tool), and used brass mounts, such as claw feet or figures, both high and low relief, in order to achieve the desired effect.

→ The Badminton Cabinet, Florence, 1695–1732. An ebony, inlaid hardwood and ormolu cabinet, with ten cedar-lined drawers inlaid with birds, foliage and flowers. It has panels of amethyst quartz, bold strips of lapis lazuli and red jasper, ormolu swags of flowers and chalcedony lion masks.

Inlay is a decorative technique where small pieces of material are inserted into accurately cut spaces on the surface of an object to form a pattern or picture. It is very often executed with wood veneers (see p.54), but shaped pieces of any suitable substance can be used in theory. Materials such as ivory, horn, tortoise shell, enamel, porcelain; and metals, such as gold, silver, copper or brass have all been inlaid on to furniture to great effect; and even pliant materials such as leather, vellum or parchment can be used.

Colourful semi-precious stones such as agate, cornelian, lapis lazuli and marble are also used for inlays, using sophisticated techniques such as mosaic, micro-mosaic, scagliola and pietra dure.

There are examples of inlay from the earliest times: ivory and bone were inlaid into Egyptian furniture, while pictorial representations in inlay have been found in Greek and Roman pieces. The earliest examples of decoration and inlays on the furniture from Mesopotamia and Egypt probably had a symbolic or magical function. The ornamentation seems to have increased as the level of functionality of the piece decreased.

Ivory, small plaques of figured marble, semi-precious stones and tortoise shell were used as costly inlays on silvered grounds in Renaissance and Baroque pieces – initially sparingly but increasingly lavishly with time. By the seventeenth and eighteenth centuries, furniture from all over Europe was extremely richly decorated with inlays of shell, ivory or metal onto wood veneers in a huge variety of patterns and pictorial images including floral motifs.

During the Rococo period, the marquetry and inlay work in France reached unprecedented levels of quality, and often formed a background for richly decorative mounts of gilded bronze and ormolu. André-Charles Boulle perfected this technique, taking it a step further by inlaying brass carvings (sometimes in combination with enameled metal) of flowers, scenes and scrolls into the wood or tortoise shell.

Inlays, particularly in metal, continued to be popular in Britain and the United States during the Neo-classical revival at the beginning of nineteenth century. Pieces by George Bullock and Charles-Honoré Lannuier are particularly identified with metal inlays. Other techniques involved the use of semi-precious stones, coloured glass and tinted marbles to create pictorially inlaid table-tops and patterned panels, giving a highly decorative finish to

← A craftsman at Mark Asplin Whiteley inlaying nickel stringing into a lacquered tabletop which will be supported by white gold fluted bases for a Gosling private client.

→ Giovanni Bagutti and Signor Plura, Scagliola at Castle Howard, 1711–12. The fireplace surround and Bacchus niche at Castle Howard, one of the earliest examples of scagliola in England.

furniture and architecture, for example the columns in the anteroom for Robert Adam at Syon House near London.

Scagliola (Ital. *scaglia*, 'chips') is a tinted, plaster-like substance created from selenite, glue and natural pigments to imitate marble and other hardstones. It can either be applied straight to an object, or used to fill the indentations of a carved-out pattern on a prepared smooth base. The dried scagliola is then polished with oil for brightness, and waxed for protection, to give rich colours and a durable surface.

Scagliola has a complex texture and depth of colour not achievable in natural veined marble. It became fashionable in the seventeenth century as a cheaper substitute for costly marble inlays, although the earliest examples originate from Roman architecture. It was imitated throughout Europe until the nineteenth century, when Italian craftsmen were brought to England to create scagliola finishes in some of the finest homes and buildings of the period. One of the earliest known examples of scagliola in England is the fireplace surround and Bacchus niche at Castle Howard, decorated by Giovanni Bagutti in 1711–12.

Scagliola's popularity continued in the United States in the nineteenth and early twentieth centuries, with examples evident in many public buildings. Although once considered an inexpensive alternative to natural stone, it is now prized for its historic value and has recently taken on something of a new lease of life, partly due to the efforts of a small number of artisan workshops who continue to perfect this craft. It is still used in modern construction as it is a plastic material which can be moulded into ornate shapes, and thus it mitigates the rising costs of quarrying and the difficulty of obtaining some colours and types of marble.

Pietra dure (Ital. 'hard stone') is the art of making intricately inlaid patterns, and often very realistic pictures, using small, carefully cut and shaped pieces of coloured hardstone. These are highly polished and fitted together to create a form of stone marquetry, often referred to as 'painting in stone'. It differs from mosaic in that the stones used tend to be smaller and not cemented together with grout, and the works themselves are generally portable. The stones are usually silicates and include coloured marbles, agates, alabaster, malachite, onyx, amethyst, jade, jasper, lapis lazuli and topaz; even precious stones can be used.

The art flourished in Florence in the late sixteenth and seventeenth centuries and is said to have originated in Italy, although it may be Indian in origin, or at least had an independent development in that country. The first pietra dure workshop in Europe seems to have been established by the Medici family in Florence in 1588, but the art was widely practiced at the courts of Naples, Madrid, Prague, Paris and elsewhere. From the late sixteenth century pietra dure was used for small objects such as cameos and bowls, and in furniture for table-tops, drawer fronts and small inlaid panels. Some of the most striking and well known examples of pietra dure can be found at the Taj Mahal, where the Mughal emperor who commissioned it, Shah Jahan, asked for precious stones to be inlaid in white marble.

The technique is skilled and labour-intensive, and involves assembling the stones in the pattern and then gluing them, stone by stone, to a support or base. The stones must be sliced into different forms, and then built up so that the contact between each section is almost invisible. The pattern is often crafted on green, white and black marble base stones and bound together by an encircling frame.

Pietra dure's popularity continued into the nineteenth century but then declined; although recently there has been something of a revival particularly in luxury decors.

Nickel stringing on a dark
stained walnut dining table,
separating the burr walnut
inlay from the main section
of straight-grain walnut.
The dining table is
supported by fluted columns
that sit on cast nickel feet.
Interior design by
Designworks, architecture
by Keppie Design.

← Rosewood with vellum
and mother-of-pearl inlay;
↑ walnut with ebony
and bone inlay; → nickel
stringing inlay surrounded
by ebony set into a Macassar
ebony sideboard.

←↑ A sycamore chaise
longue inlaid with stringing
of ebony, upholstered in
fabric by Zimmer & Rohde.

⇒ Inlay detail for a walnut
library showing the lettering
in ebony with petal leaves
in mother-of-pearl with
sandburnt leaves in burr elm.
The contrasting branches are
in burr ash and London
plane.

Accessories

↙ Antique 18th-century engraved escutcheon in brass from Bramah Locks, Romford, Essex.

One of the most challenging issues associated with the design and craftsmanship of bespoke furniture is in the sourcing of suitable hardware or embellishments: beautiful hinges, detailed escutcheons, finely made locks and tooled keys. All of these elements of detail are critical in making a piece exceptional and supporting the level of craftsmanship invested. In this Tim Gosling agrees with Gustave Flaubert, and later Mies van der Rohe, that 'God is in the details'.

When Joseph Bramah first produced his patent lock in 1784 – some fifty years before any Chubb lock, and seventy years ahead of Yale – there were an abundance of commissioning locksmiths in London. Today there are so few cabinet-makers working at the very highest level of expertise, that the demand for skilled locksmiths to produce this hardware for furniture is low, and their numbers have dwindled to almost nothing.

Bramah locks are to be found on many historical pieces of furniture spanning the last 200 years, for example the library table from Norton Hall, Nottinghamshire, by Gillows in 1814. Their distinguishing features are that the key is round, and the lock escutcheon (the mound on the cabinet face) stands proud. This escutcheon is often embellished with either engraving, or with a beaded edging or rawling.

Hand-made Bramah locks are distinguished by their structure: each internal barrel has seven slots, with seven 'sliders' that fit into these slots. On each slider, there are seven cut marks, setting the position in which the key needs to be to work the lock. The upper plate of this lock is then engraved with the company's mark (see p.162). Astonishingly there can be one unique lock setting made for the client, and just one key crafted that will open each drawer in a piece. However it is possible to make other keys that are 'set' to only open specific drawers and not others.

The design of the key is of equal importance. Again the detail that can be created is exceptional and the line between locksmith and jeweller becomes blurred, as anything is possible. Coronet designs can be hand cut to insert into the key head, or the key may even be hinged to fold into a lady's pendant locket or a gentleman's signet ring. For added detail and thoroughness, the head of the key can be stamped with the company name (see p.163).

Sourcing handles for furniture poses the same problems for the cabinet-maker as locks do, in that skilled craftsmen in this field are also scarce. There are a huge amount of inexpensive, mass-produced handles available but, as the market for bespoke pieces is so small and specialised, very few companies produce the

↓ Jean Piret (late 18th–early 19th century), Secretaire, c.1860–76. Thuya wood with gilt-bronze mounts and marble top, the interior lined with satinwood.

calibre of handles that cabinet-makers require.

Historically the handles or mounts for a piece would have been commissioned by the cabinet-makers themselves. In France, the manufacture of these pieces was divided between several guilds of skilled artisans: one to design the handle; one to make them; one to fix them onto the piece, etc. The cabinet-maker André-Charles Boulle was one of very few who could call himself both '*bronzier*' and '*ébéniste*', thanks to a royal warrant, and thus managed to avoid the complications of working with the guilds, and made his own mounts. This dual artisanship would not ordinarily have been tolerated, however, this role as '*ébéniste du roi*' for Louis XIV protected him from prosecution by the guilds.

Mounts were commonly used on furniture as a form of decoration or identification and may be left as brass mounts or gilded – the latter are commonly referred to as gilt-bronze mounts. Gilt bronze, referred to by the French as *bronze doré* or *ormolu* (Fr. *or moulu*, ground or powdered gold) is the eighteenth-century term for the finish achieved by applying finely ground gold in a mercury amalgam to a bronze object and exposing it to extreme heat until the mercury burns off and the gold remains, adhered to the object. Other objects commonly gilded in this way were small, decorative items

such as candlesticks and clocks, or mounts for porcelain. This process is also known as fire or mercury gilding (see p.128).

The earliest gilt bronze or ormolu seems to have appeared in mid seventeenth-century France with the great French designers and cabinet-makers making extensive use of the beautiful, ormolu mounts produced by master founders and finishers ('*fondeurs-ciseleurs*') such as the renowned Jacques Caffiéri, Charles Cressen, Pierre Gouthière, Pierre-Philippe Thomire in France, and Matthew Boulton in England.

Although France remained the main centre of gilt bronzing, fine examples were also produced in other countries during the eighteenth and nineteenth centuries. Genuine ormolu pieces, strictly defined as those created using traditional mercury gilding, are rare, as the practice was banned in the mid nineteenth century due to the high cost and risks to craftsmen's health (mercury gilders tended to have a relatively low life expectancy as a result of exposure to the poisonous fumes). During the late nineteenth century gilt work using the process of electrolysis became more commonplace, but these pieces were not of the same quality as traditional gilt-bronzes pieces, although they are sometimes inaccurately referred to as fire-gilded or ormolu.

← ↙ ↓ Craftsman at Bramah Locks creating the seven slots and corresponding 'sliders' on the internal barrel of a lock.

→ GOSLING stamped on the head of personalised keys.

The handles for this
mahogany chest of drawers
and dressing table by Gosling
are made in brass and nickel
plated. This gives them
weight and visual lines
against the timber. Interior
design by Joanna Trading.

←↙ This sycamore pen box is lined with pink silk velvet to hold a collection of Japanese and lacquer fountain pens. It has three lift-out trays and an inset glass panel in the lid.

→↓ A Macassar ebony twelve-winder watch box inlaid with nickel and lined in light suede. The box sits on a base that can then pivot to gain access to the six other watch winders at the back. The switches inside are designed to alternate the winding direction so that it covers the mechanical needs of all chronograph watches.

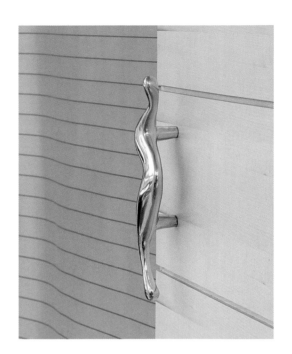

←↑ Medusa head, cast in Scotland by Farquhar Laing of Black Isle Bronze Ltd. in bronze, patinated to present a contrast against the vellum background.

↗ Polished aluminium handles, commissioned by Gosling; → in this dressing table recessed sycamore lines lined with silver leaf act as handles; ↘ handles constructed in the wood of the cabinet.

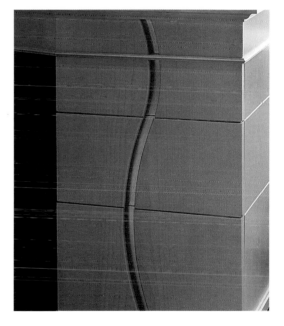

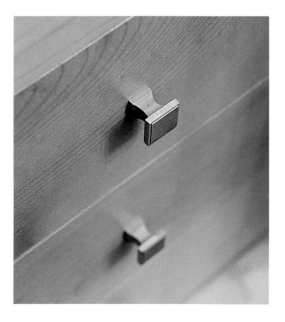

5

The Art of Technology

Furniture design has adapted throughout the centuries both to suit society's changing tastes and requirements, and in response to advances in skills of the contemporary craftsmen and designers. During the latter years of the twentieth century, however, designers have had to factor an extra element into their designs, and craftsmen expand their skill set, to allow for the ever-increasing presence of technology in our lives – not just at the office, but at home, in the study, the living room and the bedroom.

Integrating technology into our homes requires that it be housed efficiently to conceal unsightly cables and wires; to ensure optimal functioning; and to allow it to be on display when in use and completely concealed when it is not – a challenging brief especially when the environment created around it does not gel with the trappings of the twenty-first century.

Although wireless radios, gramophones and record players have all inspired designers to create furniture tailored to house, display and protect them, the advent of the personal computer, and its proliferation in our homes during the last twenty years, has had an unprecedented impact on how we design furniture to fit with our technology.

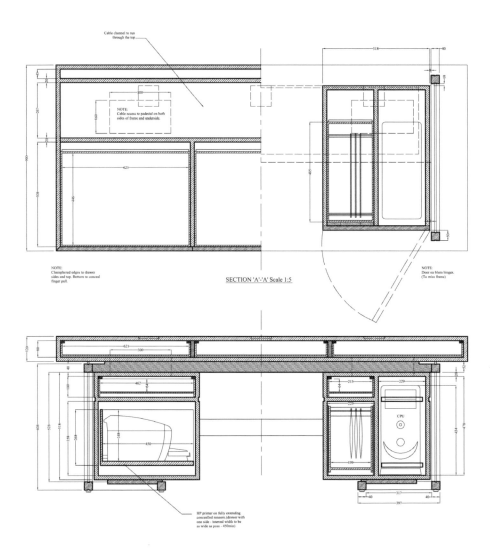

NOTE:
Cable channel to run through the top

NOTE:
Cable access to pedestal on both sides of frame and underside.

NOTE:
Chamfered edges to drawer sides and top. Bottom to conceal finger pull.

SECTION 'A'-'A' Scale 1:5

NOTE:
Door on brass hinges. (To miss frame).

CPU

HP printer on fully extending concealled runners (drawer with one side - internal width to be as wide as poss - 450mm)

→ In the modern study additional equipment such as fax machines or printers also often need to be accommodated and Gosling has used two design solutions for this storage dilemma. In the first instance the printer is stored on a pull-out, one-sided drawer in the pedestal leg – which has been enlarged to accommodate it. The design of this desk also includes management of the printer cables and power source. The pedestal desk, described in the technical drawings (◄—) showing the cable hatch and the necessary air vents to ensure adequate ventilation, was constructed in sycamore with inlay of Macassar ebony and bronze. A complete cable management system for the computer hard drive is housed within one leg of the pedestal, and a printer within the other.

←—→ The second solution is a tray system on runners that allows the printer to be tucked away between the pedestals. This pedestal desk, constructed in book-matched walnut with sycamore panels in the centre of the pedestals, is designed to integrate with the wall panelling so not only is the printer recess deceptively deep, but the lighting has been inbuilt. An added technological touch on this desk is the inbuilt cable management for use of a laptop. This particular desk was also designed to meet future evolutions – should the technology change or get smaller, this section can be removed without damaging the look or integrity of the desk.

↑ The top of the desk has a low gallery with two smaller drawers and a central panel that conceals cables and power sources for a laptop. The desktop inbuilt lighting sits on brackets fixed to the flanking cupboards.

↑→ In this pedestal desk, constructed in rosewood, the pedestals are inlaid with panels of beige shagreen and designed with complete cable management for the computer hard drive housed within. Design modifications are required to deal with the heat generated by the hard drive as this could damage both the furniture and the computer itself. Gosling tackles this problem in two ways: firstly by ensuring the pedestals have adequate ventilation but also by installing an air cooling application which draws the warm air from the hard drive. Interior design by Finchatton.

← Audio-visual technology is another area which requires integration into the design of a room or an individual piece of furniture. The replacement of large, unwieldy cathode ray monitors by lighter flat screen display panels, gives Gosling opportunities to incorporate these screens into the design of a piece of furniture, and still retain the original function of that piece. In this breakfront television cabinet in walnut with inbuilt lifting mechanism for the TV screen, the central recess between the pedestals is shallow, due to the storage space needed for the TV screen; however a mirror is inlaid in the space to make the piece seem less heavy and imposing.

↑ A television cabinet constructed in walnut wrapped in vellum, with a Medusa-head bronze mount in the central panel. The cabinet has an inbuilt lifting mechanism for the TV screen, and has cupboard sections within it for storage of media boxes, videos and other technical equipment.

More often than not, a design which allows the client to alternately display and conceal the screen on demand is needed. Streamlined, futuristic screens are jarring in more classically inspired interiors so it is essential to have them easily, and elegantly, out of sight. An example is to be found in a Georgian town house in Edinburgh, where Gosling took inspiration for the furniture throughout the house from the architecture, incorporating the Greek key motifs in the exterior railings and listed cornicing. The 42-inch Bang & Olufsen plasma-screen televisions, for all their pleasing, clean lines, aesthetically have no permanent place in this scheme. The solution was to create two credenzas, one in the breakfront style and one bowfront, which function as cabinets but also incorporate false fronts to house the television screens. Working closely with Bang & Olufsen experts Gosling created pieces where the screen rose out of the cabinet at the touch of a button on the remote control. A further design solution – the choice of a screen with an integral DVD/CD player and hard drive – eliminated the need for additional space for storage and cable management which would have compromised the size and aesthetics of the furniture.

↖ ↑ A bowfronted TV credenza, with top frieze in dark stained walnut and with inlays of Bombay rosewood.

→ A detail of the bowfronted TV credenza.

← A breakfront TV credenza, in walnut with ebony inlays, with five doors and fluted frieze.

←↑ There are, however, exceptions – times when the simplicity and geometry of the streamlined display screen integrates with and enhances a piece of furniture. This inbuilt bookcase, cantilevered off the wall to give the impression of floating, is fitted with an integral cable-managed laptop station which pulls out when in use and tucks away when not, so keeping the slimness of the piece.

→ The fitted bookcase in walnut with adjustable walnut shelves houses a 32-inch flat screen TV with full cable management.

← The art of technology is not all about boys' toys – this dressing table design by Gosling has a plug socket built into the drawer, for plugging in a hairdryer and mobile-phone charger. The dressing table is constructed in sycamore and hand lacquered with cream-coloured shellac. It has brass detailing and a shagreen inlaid top supported on eight turned and tapered legs with brass feet. The dressing-table mirror folds into the top surface and opens to reveal a compartmentalised section lined in suede.

→ The dressing table has three traditional drawers in the frieze: two on the left-hand side and a larger drawer on the right that contains a double power socket. The drawer handles are brass and turned cream lacquered sycamore. Interior design by Alidad.

Designing to accommodate technology comes into its own in office space, where almost every piece is geared toward computer or AV equipment and the challenge is to keep the space uncluttered and efficient.

The pictures below and opposite show boardroom tables designed by Gosling with audio and video conference facilities – the centres of the tables contain hinged panels to aid discreet cable management (→). The tables are constructed in sycamore with three pedestal bases with recess mouldings and acrylic detail at the bottom. The project was detailed with Christian Garnett Partners, with construction by ISG.

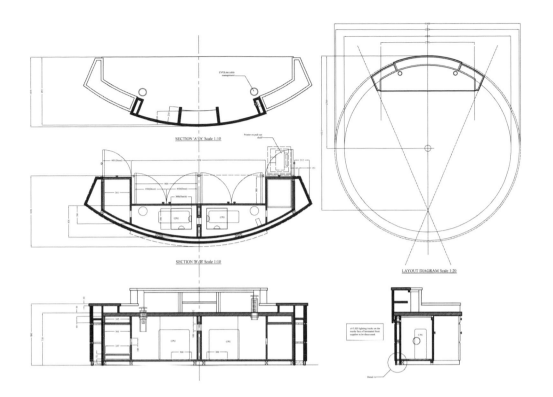

SECTION 'A'/A' Scale 1:10

SECTION 'B'/B' Scale 1:10

LAYOUT DIAGRAM Scale 1:20

A company's first impressions are created by its reception area. The design for this space needs to be clean and uncluttered – achieved in this case by creating a reception desk made up of three inbuilt pedestals which hide the computers and a printer on a pull-out drawer. Technology can, of course, add an extra dimension to design – this desk was constructed with acrylic shadow gaps between panels of the desk, and built into these are LED lights that aim to give an otherwise solid piece of furniture a lighter feel. Conventional lights would overheat and potentially damage the wood or acrylic, however the LEDs do not heat up and have a considerably longer lifespan than other lights. The reception desk is constructed in sycamore and comprises three pedestals: two for computers and one for printer, all with vents and drawer at the top of each pedestal.

← A rosewood desk with quoining lines in myrtle burr with a high gloss finish. Detail (→) showing the rosewood and myrtle burr top with cable grommets made in the same wood with matching grain direction.

6

Contemporary Design
in Classic Interiors

The architect–designers of the eighteenth and nineteenth centuries created their historic masterpieces by being involved, to a greater or lesser degree, in all aspects of a project, thus ensuring that the coherent thread of their creators' genius and inspiration runs through them. The same is true in modern schemes, which flourish when there is a coherent, integrated design process.

Technology has increased the modern designers' arsenal, allowing them to overlay different skills simultaneously and create accurate, photo-realistic plans. The other side of this coin is that allowances must be made in modern schemes for new technological requirements, not to mention adherence to rigorous planning requirements, particularly in listed buildings, and Health & Safety Regulations – all of which need to be scrupulously maintained at all times.

The biggest challenge for a modern designer working in a classical building is to avoid creating an interior, or pieces, that jar with its sensibility, and to find ways to marry the old with the contemporary without upsetting the architecture and the rhythm of the building. In recognition of the very real design risks, English Heritage (formerly the Historic Building and Monuments Commission for England and self-described as the Government's statutory adviser on the historic environment) has set up a system of

The owner of this eighteenth-century Grade I listed building in central London commissioned Gosling to design furniture and coordinate interior schemes for all the main living areas. The *pièce de résistance* of this project was the installation of a library to house a rare collection of sixteenth-, seventeenth- and eighteenth-century Venetian manuscripts.

The property had been partially renovated in the 1980s when the main water tank fell through all of the floors, destroying many of the original mouldings and irretrievably altering the house's original architecture.

The introduction of more stringent building regulations since the last renovation meant it was necessary to strip back the previous alterations, in order to create an environment more sympathetic to the origins of the building.

When dealing with buildings of such architectural importance, it is essential to have a trusted and experienced construction expert who will approach the project with sympathy and understanding for the design. In this instance ISG, a London-based firm with specialist experience working on grade listed buildings in collaboration with Tim Gosling, was entrusted with the task.

← Site work in progress on a drawing room being converted into a library in a mews house alongside a listed building in central London.

↗ Computer detail showing the working out of the relationship of the fabricated outside windows with the bookcases and the shadow of the cornices and skirting.

→ The end result – a fitted library constructed in a mews house alongside a listed building in central London. The shutters were wrapped in stamped ostrich leather with chairs upholstered in a hand-made Venetian fabric by Mario and Paola Bevilacqua.

⇒ The central door looks out towards the main house, with a soft-paste porcelain Sèvres of Karnac temple silhouetted on the table.

checks and safeguards on buildings designated as listed. When buildings are listed they are placed on statutory lists of buildings of 'special architectural or historic interest' which affords a certain amount of supervision and protection when work and alterations are planned.

Gosling's classical style, and the calibre and quality of the craftsmanship, lends itself naturally to eighteenth- and nineteenth-century environments: in 2008, over fifty per cent of the pieces and schemes created were installed in listed buildings. This means that the ability to satisfy English Heritage's listed building criteria, without compromising the design inspiration for the client, is essential. As we have learned from the historic masterpieces created in earlier centuries, creative and coherent design, well-conceived and executed in sympathy with the harmony of the building, has enduring qualities of grace and intelligence. Gosling strives to produce pieces and interiors which will, in turn, enhance the buildings in which they are created and inspire future generations.

←↑ This room has lacquered and gilded pieces by Gosling. The oil paintings of *The Four Seasons* are by Jonathon Coleman, and are spaced equally around the room. The grey shot silk curtains echo the Ionic columns in the room. The bookcase in black lacquer (→) is tapered from the dado height to the top to visually play against the plaster and grey painted grisaille columns. Interior design by Anouska Hempel Design.

↗ The double screens placed around this section of the room are filled with mirror and are lit in between them to push the light up towards the ceiling.

← A carver and a single chair by Gosling. Buttoned in the front the chairs are hand sprung, and the carver is designed with arms set back to enable the chair to sit comfortably under the frieze of its dining table.

→ A walnut club chair by Gosling with ebony feet upholstered in Pierre Frey fabrics.

← A pair of Adam shield-
back gilt chairs upholstered
in a Richard James cravat
fabric of silk, specially hand
woven to echo the Ian
Davenport oil painting that
hangs above.

→ Inspired by André Arbus,
this set of Gosling chairs is
made in lacquered sycamore
with hand-carved sabre-
legged details. The diptych
photograph of the
Royal Opera House,
was commissioned from
Alex Schneideman.

The luxury French linen house, D. Porthault, founded in Paris in the 1920s, commissioned Gosling to design this crib, inspired by elements of Fabergé's work and the shell formations at Versailles. Master craftsman Ray Gonzales of Devon took nine months to carve the crib in laminated birch, creating the striations and the strength of the piece. He then gessoed and water-gilded the crib in gold leaf.

Any planned architectural additions to a listed property must be submitted to English Heritage for approval. Such was the case with this bolection fireplace and mantelpiece designed by Gosling for the drawing room in the project. To get the required Grade I listed permission it was necessary to show that the fireplace did not detract from the original architecture and but in fact maintained a sense of character, connecting it to the 1750s building.

← Site work by ISG in progress on a living room in a listed building in central London.

↙ The end result – a living room constructed in a listed building in central London with a classical inset fireplace/mantelpiece designed and granted Grade I listed building approval by English Heritage. The fireplace is made by Jamb of London.

→ This bolection fireplace is inspired by one in Hampton Court, created in the 1690s.

≫ Fitted furniture, built into walls, is a great way to maximize space, and this library built into a Regency Grade II listed building provides an extremely compelling example of this. Despite the use of a dark wood such as walnut, fitting the bookshelves and cupboards has created a feeling of space, which is enhanced by the use of eglomise mirrors in the gables and the full-length jib doors.

Finding the balance between the English Heritage stipulations, and the designs created by Gosling and approved by the client, is not always straightforward and can involve ingenuity and lateral thinking. One such example was in a Grade I listed eighteenth-century building in central London, used as a corporation's headquarters (↓).

In order to preserve the original structure of the room used as the Boardroom, Gosling needed to find a way to install bookcases and torcheres with suspended lids, without fixing them into the listed floors or ceilings. In the example of the bookcases, this was achieved by placing heavy, stabilized bases along the floor, into which the bookcases slotted; while the torchere lids (→) were eventually suspended from extending brackets attached to the side of the wall, rather than from the listed ceiling. The electrics come up through the pedestal and shine onto the underside of the 'top hats' which are silver-leafed to reflect the light back down.

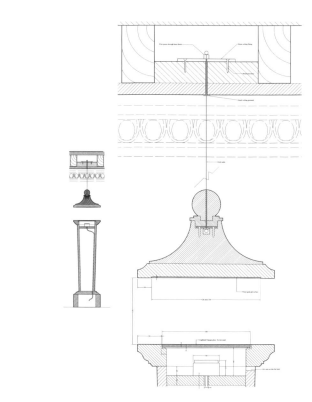

Work on historically interesting buildings can often throw up surprises in the middle of construction – not an entirely welcome prospect but one which needs to be accepted as part and parcel of the redesign of an older room. An example of this occurred during the redesign and refit of the Bar, Terrace and Lounge of the Goring Hotel, London. While installing the furniture and lighting for the Lounge, the system of electrics for the area was revealed, and it was discovered that much of this was the original wiring from the hotel's construction in 1910. As a result there were only a few, very basic circuits, not allowing for any form of individual area control. The construction company, ISG, installed new circuits, under instruction from Gosling, requiring the original parquet flooring to be torn up, which, fortunately, was soon to be covered by a Pierre Frey hand-stitched, tiger-pattern carpet (→→→). Once installed, the new system allowed for separate control of the different areas of the Bar, Terrace and Lounge, as well as the installation of dimming controls for the first time.

Keepers of the Flame: Expert Craftsmen

MARK ASPLIN WHITELEY, Yorkshire, England

A qualified wood machinist, Mark Asplin Whiteley trained at Rycotewood College, a recognised national centre of excellence, fostering ideas of craft, design, history of design and the use of materials. He has extensive experience as a cabinet maker of bespoke fine furniture, and for over twenty years, has run his own Yorkshire-based company – regarded as one of the pre-eminent British bespoke furniture workshops. Mark has a passion for fine woods and veneers; he and his craftsmen are constantly experimenting with traditional materials and innovative techniques for use in contemporary furniture.

GAVIN ROOKLEDGE, Rooks Books Ltd., London

Gavin Rookledge is one of the leading, and most adventurous, bookbinders and leather/vellum workers in the UK today. He completed a Foundation course; a BA in Expressive Arts; and a post-graduate qualification in Art and Outdoor Education. During his studies he had the good fortune to meet Faith Shannon – one of the UK's most distinguished bookbinders and a former President of the Designer Bookbinders – who became his mentor. A passion was born and he started Rooks Books in 1987, slowly taking on commissions beyond bookbinding to include vellum and leather wrapping work on all sorts of art objects, sculpture and furniture.

JÜRGEN HUBER, Senior Furniture Conservator, The Wallace Collection, London

After an apprenticeship as a cabinet maker, Jürgen Huber worked as a restorer in France, Germany and Benelux. He then became interested in all aspects of conservation and studied at the City and Guilds of London Art School, gaining a postgraduate diploma in 1998. On graduating he carried out work for public institutions and private clients in the UK, mainland Europe, Africa and the Middle East, before joining the Wallace Collection as Senior Furniture Conservator. At the Wallace Collection he is responsible for preventive and interventive conservation of furniture, clocks and related objects and has worked on decorative surfaces such as Boulle marquetry, wood marquetry, gilding, Japanning as well as Japanese lacquer, and has also re-cast or carved missing parts in wood and resins. He has also worked for other organisations as a consultant and conservator, including the World Monument Fund on the Chinese Palace at Oranienbaum in Saint Petersburg; for the Gilbert Collection; The Courtauld Institute; English Heritage; and the King Faisal Foundation in Riyadh, Saudi Arabia.

CHRISTINE PALMER, Carvers & Gilders, London

Christine is a Director of Carvers & Gilders, established in 1979, which conserves and restores fine decorative carving, furniture and mirrors. Specialists in wood carving, gesso work and gilding, their work covers a broad range of styles from traditional to contemporary for design professionals and private clients. An accredited Member of the Institute of Conservation, Christine regularly lectures in Gilding at the City & Guilds of London Art School, where she originally studied and met her fellow directors at Carvers & Gilders.

PETER BINNINGTON, Dorset, England

Peter Binnington is one of few remaining craftsmen skilled in *verre églomisé* – the ancient craft of applying and drawing on precious metal gilding on the reverse of glass panels to create shimmering effects for interiors. He has worked for over twenty years with the most renowned designers on interiors and furniture for a prestigious list of clients.

The methods he employs today are essentially the same as those used over the centuries although some more modern processes – silk-screen, ink transfer and photographic techniques – can now be used in transferring the images to the glass. Peter experiments with new processes which would allow *verre églomisé* to be used in new ways and in new contexts. Currently he is experimenting with sandwiching the gilded, etched designs between two sealed panels of glass which could then be used in showers. Some training in this ancient craft is offered by a few colleges running specialised courses in Decorative Surfaces and Peter, determined to pass on his extensive professional knowledge and experience, trains a small number of people in this art.

Contributors

TIM GOSLING graduated from the Central School of Art & Design in 1987 with a BA (Hons.) degree in Theatre Design. His work in theatre included creating set and stage scenes for major West End productions such as *Miss Saigon* and *Starlight Express* as well as working as a set designer for Las Vegas shows. His portfolio of furniture and interiors commissions includes the Savoy and Goring Hotels in London and the headquarters of British Petroleum. In the late 1980s Tim joined David Linley, becoming a director in 1993. At Linley he was instrumental in developing the company's design style and expanding their bespoke business over 18 years. In 2005 Tim set up his own company, Gosling, giving him the freedom to design a wider range of furniture and interiors while continuing his working relationships with interior designers worldwide.

STEPHEN CALLOWAY is Curator of Prints at the Victoria & Albert Museum, London. He is the author of *Baroque Baroque, The Culture of Excess, Aubrey Beardsley, Elements of Style* and *The Encyclopaedia of Domestic Architectural Details* — the most comprehensive visual survey detailing period and key styles in architecture. He writes, lectures and consults on architecture, interior design and the history of taste. He contributes regularly to a number of periodicals, including *World of Interiors, House and Garden* and *Elle Decoration*. He also writes for US periodicals, including *Architectural Digest* and *Antiques*.

RACHEL DUTHIE gained a BA in Classics at Cape Town University, after which she began working for Christie's and, latterly, Linley.

JEAN GOMM, a director of T. Gosling Ltd., is instrumental in the short- and long-term strategic development of Gosling, creating the financial blueprint that enables the company to anchor and expand Tim's creative vision. She has extensive senior executive experience in the corporate sector, international organisations and non-profit organisations, and today is a director/consultant to other companies in the creative industries and to numerous non-profit organisations. She is active in the arts and in 2007 helped organise an international exhibition on Belgian painters from the end of the nineteenth-century in Switzerland. She has qualifications in Fine Arts and MBAs from Cranfield University and Harvard Business School, and is the President of the Harvard Business School Alumni Club of London.

JÜRGEN HUBER is Senior Furniture Conservator, The Wallace Collection, London. Following the journeyman tradition Jürgen trained as a cabinetmaker and restorer in Germany, France and Benelux becoming a Tischler Meister in 1992. He gained a further degree in conservations studies in London in 1998. He has worked for public institutions and private clients in the UK, mainland Europe, Russia, Africa and the Middle East.

RAY MAIN trained as an architectural photographer but his focus has slowly changed to accommodate his other great passions of interiors, gardens, food, travel and reportage photography. His work appears regularly in magazines and over 160 books worldwide.

PHILIP STURDY, designer at Gosling, trained at Ravensbourne College of Design and Communication where he achieved a BA (Hons.) degree in Product & Furniture Design.

PHOTIS PHOTI, designer at Gosling, studied at the University of Plymouth, Faculty of Art & Design in Exeter, leaving with a BA (Hons.) degree in 3-Dimensional Design (Designer for Industry).

Selected Bibliography

'A Lost Art Found.' *Elle Décor Magazine*, February 1993.

ANSCOMBE, ISABELLE. *Arts & Crafts Style*. London: Phaidon, 1998.

Architectural Theory from the Renaissance to the Present. Cologne: Taschen, 2006.

BENTON, CHARLOTTE, TIM BENTON, GHISLAINE WOOD & ORIANA BADDELEY. *Art Deco, 1910–1939*. New York: Bulfinch, 2003.

BLAKEMORE ROBBIE G. *The History of Interior Design Furniture*. New York: Van Nostrand Reinhold, 1997.

BOURNE, JONATHAN ET AL. *Lacquer – An International History and Collector's Guide*. London: Bracken Books, 1984.

BOWE, PATRICK. *Gardens of the Roman World*. London: Frances Lincoln, 2004.

BRUNHAMMER, YVONNE. *André Arbus: Architecte-Décorateur des années 40*. Paris: Editions Norma, 2003.

BUZAS, AXEL. *Sir John Soane's Museum, London*. Berlin: Ernst Wasmuth Verlag, 1994.

CAMPBELL, GORDON. *The Grove Encyclopedia of Decorative Arts: Two-volume Set*. Oxford: Published by Oxford University Press, 2006.

CENINI, CENNINO D'ANDREA. *The Craftsman's Handbook*. Trans. Daniel V. Thompson. New York: Dover Publications, 1954.

CHASTANG, YANNICK. *Paintings in Wood: French Marquetry Furniture*. London: Wallace Collection, 2003.

CHILD, GRAHAM. *World Mirrors: 1650 – 1900*. London: Philip Wilson Publishing Ltd., 1990.

COLLARD, FRANCES. *Regency Furniture*. Woodbridge: Antique Collectors Club, 1985.

CORNFORTH, JOHN. *Early Georgian Interiors*. New Haven & London: Yale University Press, 2004.

CORNFORTH, JOHN. *Houghton Hall Norfolk*. Derby: Heritage House Group Ltd., 2007.

EDWARDS, RALPH (Preface). *Hepplewhite Furniture Designs from the Cabinet-Maker and Upholsterer's Guide*. London: Alec Tiranti Ltd., 1955 (1794).

FEDERER, FRANCES. 'Reverse Painting and Gilding behind Glass: the Story of a Nearly Lost Art, from the Late Middle Ages to the First World War.' Gilding and Decorative Surfaces Section of *Conservation News*, the Official Newsletter of United Kingdom Institute for Conservation of Historic and Artistic Works, no. 76 (November, 2001).

FLEMING, JOHN. *Robert Adam and His Circle*. Transatlantic Arts, 1978.

FOREST, TIM. *The Bulfinch Anatomy of Antique Furniture*. New York: Time Warner Book Group, 1996.

FORREY-CARLIER, ANNE. *Le Mobilier du Musée Carnavalet*. Dijon: Editions Faton, 2000.

'Glass Menagerie.' *Architectural Digest Magazine*, March 2000.

GRAHAM CHILD. *World Mirrors: 1650–1900*. Philip Wilson Publishing Ltd. 1990.

HADSUND, PER. 'The Tin-Mercury Mirror: its Manufacturing Technique and Deterioration Processes.' *Studies in Conservation*, vol. 38, no. 1 (February 1993).

HARRIS, EILEEN. *The Genius of Robert Adam: His Interiors*. New Haven and London: Yale University Press (Paul Mellon Centre for Studies in British Art), 2001.

HARRIS, JOHN AND GORDON HIGGOTT. *Inigo Jones: Complete Architectural Drawings*. New York: The Drawing Center, 1989.

HECKMANN, GUENTER. *Urushi No Waza Japanese Lacquer Technology*. Ellwangen: Nihon Art Publishers, 2002.

HEIDEMANN, E. *Fundamentals of Leather Manufacturing*. Darmstadt, Eduard Roether, 1993.

HÖFER, CANDIDA AND UMBERTO ECO. *Libraries*. Munich: Schirmer/Mosel, 2005.

HONOUR, HUGH. *Cabinet Furniture Makers and Designers*. Weidenfeld and Nicolson Ltd., 1969.

HOPE REED, HENRY. *The Works in Architecture of Robert and James Adam*. New York: Dover Publications, 1980.

HOPE, T. *Regency Furniture and Interior Decoration*. New York: Dover Facsimile Edition, 1971 (1807).

IMPEY OLIVER. *Japanese Export Lacquer: the Fine Period. Ostasiatische und Europaische Lacktechniken*. Munich: Bayerisches Landesamt für Denkmalpflege, 2000.

JACKSON, ALBERT & DAVID DAY. *Woodworker's Manual*. London: HarperCollins, 1989.

JACKSON-STOPS, GERVASE. *The Treasure Houses of Britain: Five Hundred Years of Private Patronage and Art Collecting*. New Haven & London: Yale University Press (National Gallery of Art, Washington), 1985.

JAFFER, AMIN. *Made for Maharajas: A Design Diary of Princely India*. New Holland Publishers (UK) Ltd., 2006.

JARDINE, LISA. *On a Grander Scale: The Outstanding Career of Sir Christopher Wren*. London: HarperCollins, 2002.

KEITH, GRANT W. 'Some Hitherto Unknown Drawings by Inigo Jones'. *The Burlington Magazine for Connoisseurs*, vol. 22, no. 118 (1913).

KOIZUMI, KAZUKO. *Traditional Japanese Furniture – a Definitive Guide*. Tokyo, New York, London: Kodansha International Ltd., 1986.

KRAFTNER JOHAN, TIM KNOX AND ALVAR GONZALES-PALACIOS. *The Badminton Cabinet*. Munich, Berlin, London, New York: Prestel, 2007.

KUZMANOVIC, N. NATASHA. 'The Shagreen Work of John Paul Cooper'. *Antiques Magazine*, September 1995.

LAUBIER, GUILLAUME DE & JACQUES BOSSER. *The Most Beautiful Libraries in the World*. New York: Harry N. Abrams, 2003.

LAWRENCE, SARAH E., JOHN WILTON-ELY, PETER EISENMAN, ALVAR GONZALEZ-PALACIOS & MICHAEL GRAVES. *Piranesi as Designer*. New York: Perseus Distribution Services, 2007.

MARCILHAC, FÉLIX. *André Groult – Décorateur–Ensemblier du XXe Siècle*. Paris: Les Éditions de l'Amateur, 1997.

MASSINELLI ANNA MARIA. *Scagliola – L'Atte della Pietra di Luna*. Rome: Deitalia. Editalia, 1997.

Masterpieces of the J. Paul Getty Museum – Decorative Arts. London: Thames and Hudson, 1997.

MATHESON, SYLVIA A. *Leathercraft in the Lands of Ancient Persia*. Spain: Colomer Munmany, 1978.

MAZURKEWICH, KAREN. *Chinese Furniture — a Guide to Collecting Antiques.* Tokyo, Rutland, Vermont, Singapore: Tuttle Publishing, 2006.

MCCRAY, W. PATRICK. *Glassmaking in Renaissance Venice: The Fragile Craft.* Farnham: Ashgate, 1999.

MCKITTERICK, DAVID. *The Making of the Wren Library, Trinity College, Cambridge.* Cambridge: The University Press, 1995.

MILLER, JUDITH. *Period Details Sourcebook.* London: Octopus Publishing Group, 1999.

MILLER, JUDITH, *Furniture — World Styles from Classical to Contemporary.* London: Dorling Kindersley Ltd., 2005.

MITCHELL, PAUL AND LYNN ROBERTS. *Frameworks.* London: Merrell Holberton Publishers, 1996.

MONTGOMERY-MASSINGBERD, HUGH AND CHRISTOPHER SIMON SYKES. *Great Houses of England & Wales.* London: Laurence King, 1994.

MOORE, ANDREW W. *Houghton Hall: The Prime Minister, the Empress and the Heritage.* Woodbridge: Antique Collectors' Club, Ltd., 1996.

MORGAN, MORRIS HICKY. *Vitruvius: The Ten Books on Architecture.* New York: Dover Publications, 1914.

MUNN, JESSE. 'Treatment Techniques for the Vellum Covered Furniture of Carlo Bugatti.' *The Book and Paper Group Annual,* vol. 8. The American Institute for Conservation of Historic and Artistic Works, 1989.

NAKASHIMA, GEORGE. *The Soul of a Tree: A Woodworker's Reflections.* Tokyo: Kodansha International Ltd., 1981.

OPPER, THORSTEN. *Hadrian: Empire and Conflict.* Cambridge: Harvard University Press, 2008.

PAGE, MARIAN. *Furniture Designed by Architects.* New York: Whitney Library of Design, 1980.

PARISSIEN, STEVEN. *Palladian Style.* London: Phaidon, 1994.

PERFETTINI, JEAN. *Le Galuchat.* Dourdan: Editions H. Vial, 2005.

PIERT-BORGERS, B. *Restaurieren mit Urushi: Japanischer Lack als Restaurierungsmittel.* Cologne: Museum für Ostasiatische Kunst, 1987.

PIERT-BORGERS, B. 'Aspects and problems of the application of *urushi* in the restoration of objects from European collections'. *Conservation of urushi objects: Postprints of the international symposium on the conservation and restoration of cultural property, 1993.* Tokyo: Tokyo National Research Institute of Cultural Properties, 1993.

PLINY. *Natural History.* London: Loeb Classical Library, 1952.

PORTER, TOM. *Archispeak: An Illustrated Guide to Architectural Terms.* London. Routledge, 2004.

PRADÈRE, ALEXANDRE. *French Furniture Makers: The Art of the Ébéniste from Louis XIV to the Revolution.* London: Philip Wilson (Sotheby's Publications), 1989.

RAMOND, PIERRE. *Masterpieces of Marquetry.* 3 vols. Los Angeles: J. Paul Getty Museum, 1994.

RIVERS, S. 'Removal of Varnish from Japanned and Lacquered Surfaces: Principles and Practice'. The Meeting of East and West in the Furniture Trade Sixth International Symposium on Wood and Furniture Conservation, Conference Postprints, Amsterdam: Stichting Ebenist, Rijksmuseum, 2003.

RIVERS, S. & NICK UMNEY. *Conservation of Furniture.* Oxford: Butterworth-Heinemann Ltd., 1998.

SARDAR, ZAHAD. 'Gild Complex.' *San Francisco Chronicle Magazine,* January 2002.

SCHMIDT, LEO, CHRISTIAN KELLER & POLLY FEVERSHAM. *Holkham.* Munich, Berlin, London and New York: Prestel, 2005.

STALKER, JOHN & GEORGE PARKER. *A Treatise of Japanning and Varnishing.* London: Alec Tiranti, 1960 (1688).

SUMMERSON, JOHN. *Inigo Jones.* New Haven & London: Yale University Press, 2000.

TAIT, A. A. *The Adam Brothers in Rome: Drawing from the Grand Tour.* London: Scala Publishers Ltd., 2008.

TAYLOR, ZACHARY. *Marquetry & Inlay Handbook.* New York: Sterling Publishing Company, Inc., 2003.

THOMPSON, DANIEL V. *The Materials and Techniques of Medieval Painting.* New York: Dover Publications Inc., 1956.

THORNTON, PETER AND HELEN DOREY. *A Miscellany of Objects from Sir John Soane's Museum: Consisting of Paintings, Architectural Drawings and Other Curiosities from the Collection of Sir John Soane.* London: Laurence King, 1992.

THORNTON, PETER. *Seventeenth-century Interior Decoration in England, France, and Holland.* Paul Mellon Centre for Studies in British Art. New Haven & London: Yale University Press, 1981.

THOROLD, PETER. *The London Rich. The Creation of a Great City, from 1666 to the Present.* London: Viking Penguin, 1999.

VITRUVIUS. *The Ten Books of Architecture.* New York: Dover Publications, 1960.

WARE, I. *The Designs of Inigo Jones.* London, 1731.

WEBB, M. LACQUER: *Technology and Conservation.* Oxford: Butterworth-Heinemann Ltd., 2000.

WEINREB, BEN & CHRISTOPHER HIBBERT (eds). *The London Encyclopaedia.* London: Macmillan, 1987.

WHARTON, EDITH & CODMAN JR. OGDEN. *The Decoration of Houses.* New York: W. W. Norton & Co. Inc., 1998.

WHITE, ROGER. *Chiswick House & Gardens.* London: English Heritage, 2003.

WILMERING, ANTOINE M. & OLGA RAGGIO. *The Gubbio Studiolo and its Conservation.* 2 vols. New York: The Metropolitan Museum of Art, 2000.

WILSON, MICHAEL I. *William Kent: Architect, Designer, Painter, Gardener, 1685–1748.* London: Routledge, 1984.

Works in Architecture of Robert and James Adam, The. New York: Dover Publications Inc., 1980.

WORSLEY, GILES. *Classical Architecture in Britain: The Heroic Age.* London & New Haven: Yale University Press, 1995.

ZOLLNER, FRANK. *Leonardo da Vinci: The Complete Paintings and Drawings.* Cologne: 2003.

Websites

Antique Restorers: Baggot Leaf Gilding Glossary. www.antiquerestorers.com/Articles/gold/glossary2.html

'Goat skin tradition wins the day' BBC News Nov 2, 1999. news.bbc.co.uk/1/hi/uk_politics/502342.stm

Badminton Cabinet. www.timesonline.co.uk/tol/news/uk/article401044.ece

BARBER, PHIL. *A Brief History of Illuminated Manuscripts.* www.historicpages.com/texts/mshist.htm.

KEVIN HOWEL on gilding. www.buildingconservation.com/articles/gilding/gilding.htm

CLARE STEWART. 'Reflections on the looking glass. Our correspondent explains what to look for in good antique mirrors and where to buy the finest.' www.timesonline.co.uk/tol/money/article853877.ece

Acknowledgements

I would like to thank personally all the craftsmen without whom there is no legacy: Mark Whiteley; Mark Robinson; Richard Townsend; Alan Earl; Heath Chadwick; Florian Krenn; Gareth Locker; Mike Horness; Andrew Earl; Ian Haycock; Brian Conley; Tom Jenkinson; Sam Bouvet; Bogdan Lurka; Ryan Sleightholme; Toni Hughes; Nik Conley; Walter Grievson; Martin Schaatsbergen; Chris Manship; Phil Hallam; James Jacobs; Piers Hart; Sean Sutcliffe; Ray Gonzales; Jeremy Bramah.

I would like to thank all the exceptional interior designers and architects with whom I am privileged to work: Alidad, Alidad Ltd.; Lady Weinberg, Anouska Hempel Design; Bill Bennette, Bill Bennette Design; Charlotte Neame, Charlotte Neame Interior Design; Christian Garnett, Christian Garnett Partners LLP; Lavinia Dargie, Dargie Lewis Designs; Stefa Hart, Hambleton Decorating; Joanna Wood, Joanna Trading; Kelly Hoppen, Kelly Hoppen Design; Liz Cathie, Keppie Design; John Lees, Lees Associates; Rachelaine Nahon, Lyndhurst Interiors, Anne Millais, Millais Interior Design; Nina Campbell, Nina Campbell; Charlotte Lane Fox, Prue Lane Fox; Philippa Thorp, Thorp Design; Emily Todhunter, Todhunter Earle; Michael Gallagher, Michael James Gallagher; Louis Calleja and John Nash, John Nash Antiques & Interiors; Mr. & Mrs. Carl, D. Porthault.

In particular I would like to thank: Deborah Bennett; Leonora Birt; Jonathon Coleman; Jane Dundas; Andrew Hansen; Philippa Hurd; Ruth Kennedy; Fameed Khalique; Lucie Kitchener; David Linley; Sarah Ritchie; Staci Surla Perkins; Russell Thomas; Isambard Thomas; Marianne Topham; Paul and Varda Tully; Rob Van Helden; all the many clients who have kindly allowed me to photograph both their furniture and their homes; and sincere thanks to Lord Browne for his unfailing support and patronage.

Photo Credits

Endpapers: Sketch by Tim Gosling
p.1 Detail of shagreen bar. See pp. 108–09
p.2 Detail of bedroom. See pp. 100–101
pp.4–5 Dining room. See pp. 148–49
pp.6–7 Bedroom. See pp. 164–65
pp.8–9 Sycamore House
p.10 Detail of gilded crib. See pp. 204–05
p.12 Sycamore House
p.16 Publisher's/Author's archive
p.17 Publisher's/Author's archive
p.18 By kind permission of the Master and Fellows of Trinity College, Cambridge
p.19 *left:* By kind permission of the Master and Fellows of Trinity College, Cambridge
   right: By kind permission of the Warden and Fellows of All Souls College, Oxford
p.20 By courtesy of the Trustees of Sir John Soane's Museum. Photo: Derry Moore
p.21 By courtesy of the Trustees of Sir John Soane's Museum. Photo: Geremy Butler
p.24 AKG
p.26 Publisher's/Author's archive
p.27 Publisher's/Author's archive
p.30 *left:* Publisher's/Author's archive
   right: © NTPL/Andreas von Einsiedel
p.31 © English Heritage Photo Library.
p.33 By courtesy of the Trustees of Sir John Soane's Museum. Photo: Martin Charles
p.44 *left:* By courtesy of the Trustees of Sir John Soane's Museum. Photo: Geremy Butler
   right: Publisher's/Author's archive
p.45 *left:* Publisher's/Author's archive
   right: By courtesy of the Trustees of Sir John Soane's Museum. Photo: Hugh Kelly
p.46 *top:* © NTPL/Bill Batten
p.48 *left:* Photo: Guillaume de Laubier
   right: Publisher's/Author's archive

p.55 *left:* The Metropolitan Museum of Art, Rogers Fund, 1939 (39.153) image © The Metropolitan Museum of Art
   right: By kind permission of the Trustees of the Wallace Collection, London
p.70 AKG
p.71 Photo © Holkham Estate
p.87 *left:* The Metropolitan Museum of Art, Rogers Fund, 1970 (1980.181.3) image © The Metropolitan Museum of Art
   right: ullstein bild – Roger Viollet
p.97 *left:* © Victoria and Albert Museum, London
   right: Les Arts décoratifs, Paris. Photo Jean Tholance. Tous droits réservés
pp.108–09 for the work by Tracey Emin © VG Bild-kunst, Bonn 2009
p.111 © Victoria and Albert Museum, London
p.116 By kind permission of the Trustees of the Wallace Collection, London
p.117 © Victoria and Albert Museum, London
p.127 © Victoria and Albert Museum, London
p.128 AKG
p.140 *left:* © Victoria and Albert Museum, London
   right: © The Trustees of the British Museum
p.150 *left:* By kind permission of the Trustees of the Wallace Collection, London
   right: Collections of the Prince of Liechtenstein, Vaduz-Vienna
p.151 *right:* From the Castle Howard Collection
p.161 © Victoria and Albert Museum, London
pp.222–23 Detail of shagreen. See p. 96

© The Artists for all artworks shown

Additional photography by Darren Chung

Index

*Page numbers in **bold** refer to illustrations*

Prestel Verlag
Königinstrasse 9, D-80539 Munich
+49 (0) 89 24 29 08-300
+49 (0) 89 24 29 08-335
www.prestel.de

Prestel Publishing Ltd.
4, Bloomsbury Place, London WC1A 2QA
TEL +44 (020) 7323-5004
FAX +44 (020) 7636-8004

Prestel Publishing
900 Broadway, Suite 603
New York, N.Y. 10003
TEL +1 (212) 995-2720
FAX +1 (212) 995-2733
www.prestel.com

Library of Congress Control Number: 2009927646

British Library Cataloguing-in-Publication Data:
A catalogue record for this book is available from the British Library.
The Deutsche Bibliothek holds a record of this publication in the
Deutsche Nationalbibliographie; detailed bibliographical data can be
found under: http://dnb.dde.de

Prestel books are available worldwide.
Please contact your nearest bookseller or one of the above addresses
for information concerning your local distributor.

Editorial direction: Philippa Hurd
Design, layout and typesetting: Isambard Thomas, London
Origination: Reproline Genceller, Munich
Printing and Binding: Polygraf Print spol. s r.o,
Presov, Slovakia

Printed in Slovakia on acid-free paper

ISBN 978-3-7913-4364-8 (trade edition)
ISBN 978-3-7913-6242-7 (limited edition)